Wrestling with George

and Other Tales of
Western Pennsylvania

MILES S. RICHARDS

SUNBURY
P R E S S
Mechanicsburg, PA USA

Published by Sunbury Press, Inc.
Mechanicsburg, Pennsylvania

SUNBURY
P R E S S

www.sunburypress.com

For information about special discounts for bulk purchases, please contact Sunbury Press Orders Dept. at (855) 338-8359 or orders@sunburypress.com.

To request one of our authors for speaking engagements or book signings, please contact Sunbury Press Publicity Dept. at publicity@sunburypress.com.

ISBN: 978-1-62006-302-6 (Trade paperback)

Library of Congress Control Number: 2019950636

FIRST SUNBURY PRESS EDITION: September 2019

Product of the United States of America
0 1 1 2 3 5 8 13 21 34 55

Set in Adobe Garamond
Designed by Crystal Devine
Cover by Lawrence Knorr
Edited by Lawrence Knorr

Continue the Enlightenment!

Contents

Foreword v
Introduction vii

Allaquippa, Queen of the Monongahela County . . . 1
All in a Name 5
King of the Indian Traders 7
Historic Big Sewickley Creek 10
The Intrepid Captain Gist 13
A Dunkard Disaster 17
Creating the Glades Road 21
Colonel Washington Heads Westward 24
More About Washington at Stewart's Crossing 28
The Westylvania Statehood Scheme 32
River of the Falling Banks 35
A Matter of Jurisdiction 37
A Most Valuable Commodity 41
A Most Deadly Mission 46
George Rogers Clark at Big Sewickley Creek 50
Colonel Crawford's Gruesome Death 54
George Washington's Unpleasant Western Tour . . . 58
General Putnam Comes to Simeral's Ferry 63
The Unpredictable Captain Pipe 68
Recalling Nicholas J. Roosevelt 72
The Legend of Johnny Appleseed 76
Memories of Isaac Meason 80
A Real River Man 97
A High-Quality Coal 101

Composing Along the Monongahela 104
He Hauled the Coal by Barge 108
Finding Some Strange Objects 111
A Vital Rail Link 114
Saints Along the Youghiogheny 118
A Noted Local Figure 123
Bulldozing Upon the River 128
The Distinguished Senator Cowan 131
The Battle of Buena Vista 135
A Youghiogheny River Tragedy 141
A Crime Spree by Train 144
A Most Destructive Rain Storm 149
Clairton and the Coke Industry 152
A Notable Scion of the Monongahela Valley 158

About the Author 163

Foreword

THIS MONOGRAPH covers the history of the Youghiogheny and Monongahela Rivers, Valleys from 1700 to 1900. Both rivers are among the few inland waterways globally which flow northward. During these two centuries both rivers's economies evolved from agrarian to heavy steel production. Throughout the 18th Century the rivalry between France and Great Britain for control over this region was a primary reason for the outbreak of the French and Indian War in 1754. Various British fur traders, including George Croghan and Christopher Gist, were familiar with both river valleys years before George Washington began his series of visits which will be featured within this book. Furthermore, the first English farming settlements west of the Appalachian Mountains were established along the Monongahela and Youghiogheny. The discovery of rich coal deposits in the early 19th Century ensured that coal mining replaced agriculture as the region's economic backbone. Sojourners traversed both rivers aboard vessels which ranged from canoes to steamboats. Considerable amounts of commerce traveled on these waters as well. By 1860, the appearance of rail traffic fundamentally changed transportation patterns forever. In the late 19th Century along both rivers, many tons of coal were converted into coke within circular brick ovens known as "flaming igloos." Ultimately, Henry Clay Frick combined the entire coke making process within a single large mill, the Clairton Coke Works. The coke produced at Clairton subsequently was shipped down the Monongahela to the major steel enterprises near Pittsburgh. Accordingly, the Youghiogheny and Monongahela Valleys were integrated fully into the basic steel industry.

Introduction

THE BOOK'S title is derived from an episode which occurred during George Washington's visit to the region in 1770. While attending a frontier social event at a locale in the upper Youghiogheny, he was challenged by a local rowdy to a wrestling match. Upon enduring this verbal abuse for over an hour, Washington finally obliged him with devastating results. This story is among Washington's various adventures around the Monongahela and Youghiogheny Rivers that are recounted in this book. Those two rivers are among the few natural waterways in the world which flow northward. Washington, though, was not the only notable figure to visit this area during the period between 1700 to 1900. For instance, Nicholas Roosevelt was the first scion of that notable family who became well-known in western Pennsylvania when steering one of the earliest steamboats upon the Monongahela. Moreover, the first British settlements west of the Allegheny Mountains were located along these rivers. Various of the essays within the work trace the evolution of the economy of these valleys from being an agricultural "bread basket" to a heavy industrial powerhouse, specializing in basic steel production. The list of notable local personages appearing in these pages range from the legendary "Queen" Allaquippa of the Seneca to Philander Knox, a Brownsville native, who had become a prominent corporate attorney, as well as a prominent national Republican politician by 1900.

Allaquippa, Queen of the Monongahela Country

MOST HISTORIANS of colonial Pennsyl-vania are familiar with "Queen" Allaquippa, a Native American woman living in the early 18th Century within the vicinity of the Ohio River headwaters. Around this notable woman, various legends have developed which are questionable. Many of the known facts about her, however, are also controversial. Initially, there has been speculation about her exact tribal origins. Because her name apparently is derived the Delaware [Lenape] word 'allaqueppi" which literally meant "headdress," some historians have assumed she was from that tribe. But a prominent Pennsylvania trader, Conrad Weiser, consistently identified her as a Seneca, one of the six "nations' of the Iroquois Confederation. Since Weiser had longstanding dealings with the respective western tribes, his information should be accurate.

Allaquippa probably was born, around 1700, in the western section of the colony of New York, the daughter of Oppymolleh, a Seneca chieftain of high rank. She likely migrated southward into the Upper Ohio Valley when the Seneca began to dominate that region amid the initial decades of the 18th Century. Nonetheless, she was not a "queen" in the formal sense of the title. That sobriquet was bestowed by European sojourners who noticed the significant influence she possessed among her people. Within the Iroquois Confederation, the Seneca were noted for encouraging women to play prominent roles in tribal matters. And the passing of tribal succession passed through the maternal line.

Those basic social tendencies also were enhanced in Allaquippa's case by her distinguished lineage, and an early marriage to a well-known warrior, Connodgth. In 1701, Allaquippa and her husband were among a western Indian delegation who held council with William Penn at Newcastle, Delaware. During the next four decades, therefore, she was a regular participant at the various conclaves held between the western tribes and colonial officials of both Virginia and Pennsylvania. Those two colonies were expanding into the region the British called the "Ohio Country." Accordingly, it was during the two decades prior to the French and Indian War that Allaquippa enjoyed her greatest eminence.

She was visited by a series of rival British and French envoys seeking to secure her friendship. Those various emissaries generally found her living in different locales. For instance, in 1748, Conrad Weiser located her in a village upon the Allegheny River several miles above the confluence with the Ohio River. Two years later the French soldier Captain Celeron de Blainville met her at Logstown, a major Indian village at the nexus of the Ohio River and Chartiers Creek. She reportedly was living there with her sister and brother-in-law, Peter Chartiers, a noted fur trader. An indication of her stature around Logstown is that nearby Brunot's Island was known as Allaquippa's Island during the colonial period.

By 1753, Allaquippa had relocated to an encampment near the mouth of the Youghiogheny River where the city of McKeesport now stands. She and her followers probably chose this site to be closer to their vital corn supply which was grown further upriver at a locale then known as "Allaquippa's Cornfield." Located in modern North Huntingdon Township it is now called Robbins Station. This broad field of fertile bottom land was the destination of sojourners traveling over one branch of the Nemacolin's Path, a major Indian trail.

Allaquippa was living at her Youghiogheny village in 1753 when George Washington and Christopher Gist passed through the region during their famous mission to Fort Le Boeuf, the French bastion near Lake Erie. On the return journey, Washington again met with Allaquippa and presented her with a "match coat" and a bottle of rum.

Because Allaquippa ultimately chose to back the British, in 1754, her position became dangerous when the French established Fort Duquesne at the Ohio River's headwaters. Fearing attack by the French soldiers and their Native American allies, she was among a group of fugitives that fled southward to gain protection from George Washington's small Virginia militia force encamped nearby the Youghiogheny River at Great Meadows. Subsequently, Allaquippa, and her companions proceeded eastward through the Allegheny Mountains toward the perceived safety of the Pennsylvania eastern frontier settlements.

Upon reaching their destination, Allaquippa, with her relatives settled down at George Croghan's fortified estate of Aughwick, which was near the modern town of Shirleysburg. Croghan was a leading fur trader and tireless land speculator. In any case, Croghan had known Allaquippa for many years due to his numerous western trade junkets. She lived the remaining months of her life at Aughwick. The rigors of the exile journey apparently had been too much for the elderly woman. Accordingly, she was deceased by December 1754. Croghan mentioned her death within a letter, dated December 23, to a

Philadelphia business associate. He also stated that Allaquippa had been buried upon the estate.

Although "Queen" Allaquippa has been dead for nearly three centuries, her historical fame within the region has not diminished. Over the years her name was bestowed upon various geographic locations, notably the city of Aliquippa in Beaver County. The facts that details of her life are still debated by modern historians indicates she still asserts a presence within western Pennsylvania.

All in a Name

THROUGHOUT THE early decades of the 18th Century European fur traders, notably Conrad Weiser and George Croghan, regularly traveled into western Pennsylvania. During these sojourns, they encountered a river flowing northward out of Virginia, which the Native American tribes called the Yohogania {Youghiogheny]. For the next 300 years, numerous people have speculated about the origins of this name.

When drawing a frontier regional map in 1751, a Virginia militia officer, Captain Joshua Fry, specifically highlighted the *Youywagany* River. The river also appeared within other extant colonial documents featuring a wide variety of spellings. The current form of Youghiogheny generally was accepted by the Civil War period. But the popular nickname the [Yoh] Yough has been around since colonial times. Not surprisingly, many persons, including George Washington and Thomas Jefferson, speculated about the exact translation of the river's name

Apparently, *gheny* was a Shawnee word denoting "flowing water." A prominent western traveler, John Heckwalder, fluent in several Native American tongues, asserted that the name meant "winding stream." A later Pennsylvania folklorist, Franklin

Cowan, wrote that the initial translation was "river of blood." There is a quirky theory, however, which makes for a good story.

Amid the French and Indian War [1754-1763] a white fur trapper was inspecting his traps at some point along the Youghiogheny's western bank. He became disconcerted, though, upon discovering that a Native American warrior [possibly Shawnee] was watching him from the opposite shore. After exchanging hasty, wild shots, both men sought the nearest cover. As the trapper dove into a thicket, his adversary took shelter behind a large elm tree. Subsequently, they traded gunfire at least three times. Following each exchange, the Native American emerged into full view, brandishing his musket and tomahawk He also yelled derisively, "Yoh! [Yough], Yoh! Yoh."

The warrior always ducked behind the elm after concluding this curious ritual. During a quiet interlude, lasting several hours, the trapper remained out of sight. Consequently, his enemy surmised that he was either dead or had departed the area. The warrior eventually emerged from his shelter and approached the river bank. A bullet from the trapper's musket promptly passed through his neck, with fatal results. Upon staggering several feet, the stricken warrior toppled into the river. While watching the body floating away, the jubilant victor shouted, "Maybe you'll, *Yoh again eh.*" At least that was how this tale has been told.

King of the Indian Traders

AMONG THE various European adventurers who traveled beyond the Allegheny Mountains after 1720, no one became more associated with the region than George Croghan, the so-called "King of the Indian Traders." For over forty years, he was involved in most of the major events that occurred around the Upper Ohio Valley. He was among the first British observers to appreciate the potential of the lands beyond the Appalachians.

He was a persistent advocate that the British colonies create strong ties with the respective Native American tribes. Consequently, the governments of Virginia and Pennsylvania utilized his services at all the Anglo-Indian councils held prior to 1755. Unfortunately, though, his penchant for securing large personal land grants from the Indian leaders during those conclaves earned him the lasting distrust of prominent leaders in both colonies.

Croghan never hesitated to admit his intention of being the foremost land proprietor west of the mountains. Most of his private transactions were made with the main sachems of the Iroquois Confederation. By 1755, he purportedly possessed 200,000 acres around the Ohio River headwaters. Among these landholdings was a tract of 30,000 acres along the Youghiogheny adjacent to Big Sewickley Creek's mouth. After 1747, Croghan resided upon a fortified estate, Aughwick, which stood on the Susquehanna River near Harris Ferry [Harrisburg]. But the advent of major French expansion into the Upper Ohio Valley in 1748, forced him to delay any plans to develop those frontier holdings.

By 1757, Croghan was offered a key British imperial post under Sir William Johnson, the Superintendent of Indian Affairs for North America [Northern Department]. As Johnson's chief deputy, in 1758, Croghan accompanied Brigadier General John Forbes in his successful campaign to capture Fort Duquesne, the major French bastion at the Ohio River's headwaters. For the next decade, Croghan operated out of Fort Pitt and resided in the nearby village of Pittsburgh.

Throughout these years, he continued his plans to create a personal western proprietorship. He intended to have the respective tracts developed by tenants who would be paying annual rents to his land agents. Moreover, Croghan was to claim a yearly percentage of the profits derived from the commodities produced on the tenants' farms.

Meanwhile, important politicians in Pennsylvania, and Virginia were determined to drive Croghan from the frontier region. Through the influence of Joseph Galloway and John Dickinson, in 1771, the Pennsylvania Colonial Assembly voided Croghan's major Indian land grants, Furthermore, Croghan was informed that the Virginia House of Burgesses planned to follow suit.

Interestingly, the intense preoccupation with western matters had caused Croghan to pay scant attention to the growing American rift with Great Britain Accordingly, the outbreak of the American Revolutionary War, in April 1775, found him unprepared. His renowned skill at political survival, therefore, failed him at this point. The popular belief spread around

Pittsburgh that Croghan was a Loyalist. And many creditors began calling in longstanding financial obligations. By March 1777, Pennsylvania officials foreclosed on his real properties within western Pennsylvania.

To avoid bankruptcy Croghan was forced to sell off his remaining possessions in the Ohio Valley. By 1778, he had moved back to Philadelphia and was living with a married daughter. Although often denounced as a Loyalist, the patriots periodically sought his help on assorted frontier matters. For instance, in 1777, George Rogers Clark solicited Croghan's advice while preparing for his daring military expedition into the Northwest Territory.

Nevertheless, the impoverished Croghan barely escaped being imprisoned for debt. By 1780, virtually all his frontier properties, therefore, long since had been sold. Subsequently, as late as 1830, Croghan's heirs were initiating litigations to regain portions of their lost inheritance. Following a long illness George Croghan died, on August 31, 1782, within a small rented cottage in Philadelphia.

Historic Big Sewickley Creek

THE NAME of "Sewickley" is quite familiar to all western Pennsylvania residents since it has been bestowed upon various geographic entities throughout the region. One waterway in Westmoreland County is known as Big Sewickley Creek, the mouth of which empties into the Youghiogheny River about three miles below the town of West Newton. For the record, several miles inland a smaller stream known as Little Sewickley Creek flows westward toward Irwin, Pennsylvania

Sewickley is derived from the Shawnee word, *The-weg-ila* [Turtle], a surname for one of the five major tribal clans. According to Shawnee tradition, moreover, the principal tribal chieftain usually was selected from the Sewickley Clan. An Indian trader from Philadelphia, Jonas Davenport, in October 1731, came upon a Native American village located at the mouth of the creek. He discovered that the families living there were Sewickley Shawnee. Accordingly, he began calling the town "Sewickley Old Town," He further reported that the encampment was defended by a score of warriors led by Chief Aquilma. Almost an afterthought he decided to name the adjoining stream, Sewickley Creek. In any case, "Sewickley Old

Town" had been abandoned, by 1749, when George Croghan claimed the site.

Apparently, in August 1749, the high chieftains of the Iroquois Confederation, the purported overlords of the Upper Ohio River, had granted 200,000 acres of land to Croghan. Within this vast real estate was a landholding of 60,000 acres spanning both banks of the Youghiogheny for five distance miles on either side of Big Sewickley Creek. At the creek's mouth, Croghan established a storehouse [trading post] which he called Oswegle Bottom. By 1754, Croghan was storing an inventory of beaver furs at Oswegle annually worth 300 L [pounds]. This estimate was included, in April 1754, within a business statement Croghan sent to Philadelphia trading associates. Three employees evidently were stationed permanently at this storehouse to protect the property, and supervise the local fur trade around the Youghiogheny. Not surprisingly, Oswegle Bottom was abandoned, in July 1755, amidst the widespread panic among British frontier settlers following Major General Edward Braddock's disastrous defeat. Croghan's employees, therefore, decamped upon hearing reports that a French-Indian war party from Fort Duquesne was heading their way.

As the French and Indian War was concluding Croghan again became interested in his Youghiogheny River real properties. By 1762, near the old storehouse, he had established a farm where his partner, Colonel William Clapham of Pittsburgh, took up residence. A contingent of white workers was hired to develop the Big Sewickley Creek tract for future settlement. Croghan also brought in livestock, notably cattle, which were quartered in pens near the farmhouse. Some of the workers were slated to become Croghan's tenant farmers. Unfortunately, though, "Pontiac's War" thoroughly ruined this careful plan. In 1763, the western Indian tribes, led by the charismatic Ottawa chieftain,

Pontiac, suddenly attacked British frontier settlements in the Ohio Valley. During the evening of May 25, 1763, a Delaware war party raided Croghan's Youghiogheny "plantation" with devastating results. These raiders systematically burned the farmhouse and all other buildings. They murdered Clapham and several workers, and slaughtered all the livestock. The survivors fled to the comparative safety of Fort Pitt.

Consequently, in the decade following this disaster, Croghan did nothing with his Youghiogheny lands. During this period various settlers moved in around Big Sewickley Creek to establish their own farms. Although legally squatters, Croghan made no effort to dislodge any of them. He also began to sell most of his western Pennsylvania properties to pay off heavy financial debts. By 1776, he sold much of his Big Sewickley Creek acreage to a major creditor, Bernard Gratz, a Philadelphia merchant. The modern hamlet of Gratztown, not far Big Sewickley Creek's mouth, is named after this individual. George Croghan's downfall marked the end of the early period Big Sewickley Creek's history.

The Intrepid Captain Gist

CHRISTOPHER GIST was born, in August 1706, on a farm near Baltimore, Maryland. As a surveyor, his father, Richard Gist, had assisted in plotting Baltimore's initial town layout. Subsequently, the elder Gist trained his son in the surveying business. By 1738, Christopher Gist had married Sara Howard and was living in Roanoke, Virginia. He also acquired a land tract along the Yadkin River in North Carolina. In 1751, a Virginia land speculating enterprise, the Ohio Company, hired Gist and Thomas Walker to explore, and map the large territory surrounding the Ohio River. British residents along the Atlantic seaboard called this unknown region the "Ohio Country."

Initially, the pair traveled upon the old Native American trail through the mountain between the respective headwaters of the Potomac and Monongahela Rivers. They ultimately followed the Monongahela to its confluence with the Allegheny River. The explorers proceeded down the Ohio River Valley toward Kentucky. They surveyed all the countryside to the Great Miami River in western Ohio. Upon crossing the river at the "Great Falls" [Louisville] they traveled through Kentucky to the Cumberland Gap. Accordingly, Gist and Walker had traversed Kentucky two decades prior to Daniel Boone.

Throughout most of 1752, the pair undertook a second journey beyond the Allegheny Mountains and performed a systematic survey of western Pennsylvania and northwest Virginia. Apparently, Gist was careful to note the rich bottomland along the Youghiogheny River. During this expedition, they became aware that French operatives were active within the region. In fact, French officials in Quebec had hired some Indian warriors to murder them.

Nonetheless, upon returning to Williamsburg, Gist made plans to resettle in western Pennsylvania. A business partner, William Cromwell, already had recruited eleven families to reside upon Gist's landholding, later know as Mount Braddock in modern Fayette County. This land tract was situated between the Youghiogheny and Monongahela. Although several isolated settler cabins probably existed in 1753. Gist's settlement was the first organized farming community west of the mountains.

Despite his activities at Mount Braddock, Gist agreed to accompany George Washington to Fort Le Boeuf, a French outpost nearby to Lake Erie. Washington was carrying a letter from Governor Robert Dinwiddie of Virginia to the appropriate French authorities. They reached their destination by following the Venango Path, which Gist knew from earlier sojourns. Although Captain de Saint Pierre listened politely, he curtly dismissed Dinwiddie's demand to evacuate Fort Le Boeuf. Throughout the return journey, Gist and Washington endured frigid temperatures. And Gist reportedly saved Washington's life at least twice.

By April 1755, a large French military force had arrived at the forks of the Ohio. They proceeded to construct a formidable bastion, Fort Duquesne. Gist apparently made several scouting trips to monitor French military activities. At the end of May Washington commanding 180 militia troops had reached Great Meadows, an open terrain between Laurel Hill and Chestnut

Ridge. On May 27, Gist rode over to Washington's Great Meadows camp. He reported that about fifty French troops, under Ensign Coulon de Jumonville, were somewhere near his settlement. Moreover, while riding over he had spotted their tracks a couple of miles from Great Meadows. Gist, though, did not stay to participate in Washington's night attack at Jumonville's Glen.

During the early summer of 1755, Gist was performing scout duty for the British expeditionary force, under General Braddock, marching northward from Virginia. The goal of the campaign was to capture Fort Duquesne. During the march, the British also were constructing a military roadway, later known as Braddock's Road. The route partly was based upon survey maps once prepared by Gist. On several occasions, Gist's presence forestalled some tense physical confrontations between British regulars and their Iroquois allies. Following the deadly ambush at Turtle Creek, upon the Monongahela River, Gist assisted Washington in providing cover for the retreating army. By late the next afternoon, some of the fleeing soldiers already had reached the Youghiogheny some forty miles from the battlefield.

By nightfall, on July 10, the battered remnants, including a dying Braddock, had reached Gist's settlement. But an enemy raiding party already had burned all the buildings. Gist was relieved to hear later that the settlers, including his family, had fled to Maryland before the attack. For the next eight months, Gist commanded a ranger squad composed of volunteers from Maryland and Virginia. Besides monitoring French military activities around Fort Duquesne, they intercepted several raiding parties seeking to attack frontier communities on the eastern side of the mountains.

By June 1757, Captain Gist had been dispatched to the Carolinas to secure an alliance between the British and Cherokee. And he was designated as a special British agent with the other southern Native American tribes, notably the Catawba and Choctaw. Otherwise, Gist's later activities, and whereabouts are unclear. He apparently never returned to western Pennsylvania during his final years. He was reported to have died in South Carolina of smallpox in 1759. Another account, however, maintains that Gist had retired to a farm near Cumberland, North Carolina. After living in obscurity for more than three decades, in 1794, he passed away. This event apparently went unnoticed in Pennsylvania.

A Dunkard Disaster

RELIGIOUS COMMUNAL settlements were an integral aspect of American frontier history for two centuries. Among the earliest of such communities were those created in Pennsylvania by the German Pietistic [Protestant] sects. Moreover, the initial settlement of this type within the western side of the Appalachian Mountains, in 1751, was originally meant to be created along the lower Youghiogheny River. These intentions, though, were thwarted and construction began at another locale further south upon a tributary creek leading into the Monongahela River. The settlers of this community belonged to the Church of the Brethren and commonly were called "Dunkards." Their wilderness commune survived peacefully for several years until the outbreak of the French and Indian War in 1754.

The sobriquet of "Dunkard" was derived from the sect's ritual practice of baptism by immersion. Although they established several congregations around eastern Pennsylvania, notably the Ephrata Cloister in Lancaster County, the bulk of the members attended the main church in Germantown. By 1746, one group moved southward along the Appalachians to the New River Valley of Virginia. Their goal was to create a frontier agricultural settlement patterned after Ephrata Cloister.

Furthermore, they decided this community should be located beyond the mountains within the "Ohio Country." Their acknowledged leader, Samuel Eckerlein, by 1751, had scouted the region thoroughly, and decided a good site would be upon the Youghiogheny nearby to Big Sewickley Creek's mouth.

Accordingly, on May 25, 1751, George Croghan recorded within his daily journal that a "Dunkard from Virginia" had arrived in Logstown, a major Indian village on the upper Ohio River. This nameless sojourner almost was Eckerlein. And he quickly sought out Scarouady, the Seneca chieftain who oversaw the Upper Ohio Valley for the Iroquois Confederation. At a council with Scarouady and other local leaders, he requested formally their assent to the founding of the Youghiogheny settlement. In any case, Scarouady informed him that it was not in his power to grant such requests. All authority in such matters was possessed solely by the Onondaga Council, the Iroquois Confederation's governing body. He also advised Eckerlein to approach Lieutenant Governor James Hamilton of Pennsylvania in Philadelphia. Apparently, Pennsylvania governors were known to negotiate such land deals with the Onondaga Council on behalf of private interests. There is no indication, though, that this course was followed, because every Dunkard knew that Hamilton despised their sect.

Although probably a coincidence that Croghan was in Logstown when Eckerlein arrived, he was not a neutral observer. Accordingly, Croghan likely pressured Scarouady to decline the request. At that point, Croghan possessed extensive real property along the Youghiogheny, especially around Big Sewickley Creek. Croghan had definite plans for the settlement of that specific locale which he intended to supervise personally. He obviously had no desire to see a community of independent Dunkards anywhere near his property

Despite this setback, Eckerlein did lead his fellow Dunkards northward from Virginia in 1752. Instead of heading to the Youghiogheny, though, they settled upon a site along a tributary stream of the Monongahela River within modern Greene County, Pennsylvania. Subsequently, this waterway became known as Dunkard's Creek.

Interestingly, the Dunkard's Creek settlement existed for two years after General Braddock's disastrous defeat in July 1755. The French military authorities at Fort Duquesne initially took no notice of their presence within the region. Knowing that an attack probably was inevitable, however, the settlers took the advice of a friendly Delaware warrior and moved to a spot upon the Cheat River, within modern West Virginia.

By August 1757, Captain François de Lignery, the Fort Duquesne commandant, finally ordered the destruction of the Dunkard settlement. Late one night a party of French and Indian raiders launched their attack upon the hapless Dunkards. The raiders burned down all the buildings, destroyed the crops, and killed many of the settlers. The survivors were marched to Fort Duquesne where they were confined to the stockade under harsh conditions. A devout Catholic, Captain de Lignery had scant sympathy for these religious "heretics." Subsequently, he turned over most of them to his western Indian allies. But some of the captives were transported to other prisons in Canada. Among these unfortunate prisoners, only Johann Schilling escaped his Shawnee captors, in 1760, and returned to Philadelphia.

At the time of the attack, Eckerlein had been away in Winchester, Virginia on a trading junket. After learning of this tragic event, he returned to eastern Pennsylvania. While alive for two more decades he never revived the effort of establishing a religious communal settlement beyond the Appalachian Mountains. Although this initial frontier religious community came to a violent conclusion, the project was not a total failure. The Dunkard's Creek settlement did flourish for several years. Without the advent of the French and Indian War, this settlement may have existed indefinitely. The Dunkards' ultimate destruction did not discourage other religious groups from initiating similar communal efforts beyond the Appalachians throughout the next century.

Creating the Glades Road

ON APRIL 3, 1764, at the written request of Lord Thomas Penn, the proprietor, the Pennsylvania Colonial Assembly declared that much of the colony's lands west of the Allegheny Mountains would be open for settlement. Those specifically designated were tracts directly owned by the Penn family. Prospective settlers would be permitted to acquire 300 acres at a cost of 18 pounds [sterling]. Subsequently, they were required to pay an annual quitrent of one shilling to the proprietary agents. Special provisions also were made for the numerous "tomahawk claimants" currently living upon much of this acreage. Any settlers who had had already made tangible improvements upon their landholdings were to be given the initial purchase right.

Enough settlers, by late 1771, had emigrated beyond the Allegheny Mountains to warrant the creation of a new Pennsylvania county. Accordingly, in January 1772, the colonial legislature created Bedford County, the first such new jurisdiction in over a decade. The geographic boundaries included the region around the Ohio River's headwaters. Furthermore, Bedford County was sub-divided into several townships. The most western of these entities was named Rostraver Township. Within the Quarterly Session Docket of Bedford County Court, it was described as follows: "Beginning at the mouth of Jacobs Creek and running down the Youghiogheny River where it joins the Monongahela River; then up the Monongahela to the mouth of Redstone Creek, and then with a straight line to the said beginning."

Among the first actions of the Bedford County Quarterly Court was authorizing the construction of a new road running westward from the town of Bedford to the Youghiogheny River. The court was acting upon the petition of several landowners living along Big Sewickley Creek. They had stated: "We labor under great hardship and inconvenience for want of a road from . . . Bedford to the glades of the Yough and Stony Creek and by Sewickley Creek to the said river." Consequently, on July 14, 1772, the Quarterly Court appointed four commissioners to supervise this important road construction project. By September 10, a surveying party had completed laying out the designated route.

From Bedford, this roadway was to traverse over Laurel Hill, and Chestnut Ridge. Ultimately, the road was to conclude "at the thirty-one tree [mark] from Fort Pitt on Braddock's Road where the courses of Sewickley Creek converge." By October 14, work parties were systematically constructing a road that was "sixty miles long and thirty-three feet wide." This road clearly was the revival of a wilderness route designated seventeen years earlier by James Burd and George Croghan.

But Croghan, now a Pittsburgh resident, was not pleased with this development. For twenty years he had been claiming ownership over most of the acreage surrounding Big Sewickley Creek's mouth. This landholding had been granted to him by the Iroquois Confederation. Pennsylvania officials, however, consistently refused to accept the validity of Croghan's Indian land grants. Accordingly, he realized that this new roadway ensured that any plans to develop that area for his personal profit would be forestalled permanently.

In any case, the existing residents of Rostraver Township benefited from this new roadway, which became known as the Glades Road. And the artery clearly enhanced the goal of solidifying the links between eastern Pennsylvania and Pittsburgh. Moreover, the Glades Trail became an important route for sojourners heading for the Upper Ohio Valley. In the early 21st Century this roadway is known as Route 31 to motorists heading westward toward West Newton.

Colonel Washington
Heads Westward

THROUGHOUT 1770 George Washington had been encountering major financial problems at his plantation, Mount Vernon. Two years of poor harvests had forestalled his efforts to make any meaningful profit. And some costly renovations to the main house were depleting his cash reserves. Almost daily he was receiving correspondence from creditors, especially in Great Britain. For several years he had been engaging in extensive frontier land speculation beyond the Allegheny Mountains. By July 31, Washington made it known that he would be traveling to Pittsburgh that autumn.

This was his first sojourn into western Pennsylvania since 1758, amid the French and Indian War. During that conflict, Washington had achieved the rank of colonel within the Virginia colonial militia. Accordingly, at this juncture, he usually was referred to as Colonel Washington. Three years earlier Washington had contacted an old militia associate, Captain William Crawford, who was living at New Haven Farm, a plantation upon the Youghiogheny River in western Pennsylvania. He owned much of the acreage where the modern town of Connellsville was established. Subsequently, Crawford had become Washington's personal land agent, authorized to designate, survey, and purchase any real property on his client's behalf.

By late August, Washington was ready to travel westward and inspect Crawford's handiwork. Prior to departing, though, Washington met with various other active Virginia land speculators in Fredericksburg, Virginia. He agreed to inspect personally, when possible, their respective land claims. He departed Mount Vernon, on October 5, accompanied by his longtime friend, Dr. James Craik, along with three anonymous African American male slaves. Among this unknown trio was Billy Lee, Washington's personal valet. As the historian Hugh Cleland has written: "As the bright autumn hues appeared among the forests of the Blue Ridge . . . George Washington set out . . . for lands he had fought to win and now . . . to own."

At Staunton, Virginia, the travelers were joined by Crawford's brother, Valentine. They made a stopover in Oldtown, Maryland to visit with Colonel Thomas Cresap, a colorful frontier figure. On October 12, Washington's party traversed the Great Crossing of the Youghiogheny River, a major river ford within modern Fayette County, Pennsylvania. After traveling over Laurel Hill an enthusiastic Washington described the surrounding countryside as "charming." Within his daily journal, he also noted that the Youghiogheny bottom lands possessed soil "as rich and black as anything possibly be." Interestingly, Washington consistently spelled the river as *Youghyoughgane*.

About 5:00 P.M., on October 13, the travelers reached New Haven Farm. Due to a nearby ferry, that locale was known then as Stewart's Crossing. While inspecting the farm Washington declared that his host's lands were "very fine." The next morning Crawford showed his guests a local coal mine. Washington remarked that the soft coal "seemed to be of the . . . best kind, burning freely [with] an abundance of it." Nonetheless, he did not choose to invest in any coal mining operation.

Instead, the next day, Washington and Crawford rode twelve miles to view a tract of 1200 acres. A year earlier Crawford had purchased this acreage that became known as Washington's Bottom {Perryopolis]. Washington declared this landholding "as fine a land as ever I saw, a great deal of (it) rich bottom land." He also noted, "This tract is well watered and has a valuable Mill Seat." He agreed, therefore, to hire a Virginia expatriate, Gilbert Simpson, to manage a new grist mill. Washington apparently ignored a local settler's warning that the nearby stream [Washington's Run] usually became too shallow during droughts. By 1774, the mill had become operational under Simpson's direction. Unfortunately, though, throughout the coming years, Washington gained little profit from this investment.

After this inspection, Washington returned to New Haven Farm. At sunrise, on October 17, Washington and several companions, including the Crawford brothers, began riding on horseback northward along the Youghiogheny's northern bank toward Pittsburgh. Approximately ten miles from Budd's Ferry they passed by Big Sewickley Creek, Within three hours these sojourners reached the confluence of the Youghiogheny and Monongahela Rivers [McKeesport]. At that point, he may have met an old acquaintance, David McKee, the earliest settler within that locale.

Upon fording Turtle Creek, they encountered Braddock's Field, the battlefield site of the catastrophic British defeat, in July 1755. Apparently, Washington was not inclined to recall personally painful past episodes. He did express, though, satisfaction at discerning "a great deal of exceeding fine land," notably between the Big Sewickley and Turtle Creeks. Always the careful observer, Washington calculated that "43½ Measured Miles" separated New Haven Farm from Fort Pitt. After reaching their destination that evening, the sojourners took lodging at Samuel Semple's tavern. The village of Pittsburgh stood approximately three hundred yards from Fort Pitt. For the next three days, they enjoyed the hospitality of various leading Pittsburgh residents, including George Croghan.

On October 20, Washington and seven companions climbed into a large canoe and rowed down the Ohio, bound for the nexus with the Muskingum River. Initially, Washington planned to be back at Crawford's home by November 14. But he chose to survey several additional large tracts farther down the Ohio River. Consequently, his party did not return to Pittsburgh until the third week of the month. Following two days of rest, Washington's party departed Pittsburgh. A heavy snowstorm forced them to seek shelter within Widow Myers's tavern at Turtle Creek. Two days later they found that the Youghiogheny was too high at Stewart's Crossing to use the ferry. Somehow, they eventually procured a boat to make the crossing.

Although additional snow storms made traveling difficult, on December 1, Washington safely reached Mount Vernon "after an absence of nine weeks and one day." Meanwhile, he had claimed another 50,000 acres of frontier real estate. Believing that these properties were important to his finances, Washington also planned to undertake regular western tours. Within five years, however, he would be drawn into the American Revolutionary War. Accordingly, he did not return to his western Pennsylvania properties for another fourteen years.

More About Washington at Stewart's Crossing

ON OCTOBER 5, 1770, George Washington departed from Mount Vernon Plantation in Virginia, bound for the western frontier beyond the Allegheny Mountains. His primary companion was his longtime friend, and personal physician, Dr. James Craik, who usually went along on such sojourns. Once beyond the mountains, Washington would be inspecting personally the extensive lands he owned within that region. Awaiting Washington's arrival was Captain William Crawford, his land agent since 1768. Crawford's plantation, New Haven Farm, was situated upon the Youghiogheny River, directly opposite from Stewart's Crossing, where a ferry operated.

Upon reaching Fredericksburg, Virginia, the sojourners were joined by the land agent's brother, Valentine Crawford. By October 13, they were riding through Great Meadows, the site of Washington's earlier exploits amid the French and Indian War. Interestingly, Washington made no mention of this fact within his daily journal. He apparently was not inclined to recall such events in later years.

After crossing over Laurel Hill, they made a stopover at Thomas Gist's farm. Fifteen years earlier his father, Christopher

Gist, had been Washington's associate in several frontier adventures. Thomas Gist was living on his father's old property of Mount Braddock, the site of the first British settlement west of the Allegheny Mountains. Within his journal, Washington described the surrounding countryside as "charming," along with possessing abundant white oak trees. He also noted the soil "in spots [was] exceeding Rich, and in general free of stones."

By 5:00 P.M., on October 13, the travelers had reached New Haven Farm, which Washington believed "possessed some very fine bottom land" along the Youghiogheny. Early the next morning he toured a nearby coal mine which impressed him favorably. But he chose not to invest in any local coal mining enterprise. Washington and Crawford subsequently rode twelve miles to Washington's Bottom [Perryopolis], where the former already owned sizeable real estate. While at that locale Washington made plans to establish a grist mill.

Upon arriving back at New Haven Farm, they discovered that Colonel Adam Stephen was awaiting them, He was another prominent Virginian who had purchased several large Youghiogheny land tracts. Being an old friend from the French and Indian War, Washington was happy to have Stephen's company for the next several days.

Meanwhile, Washington's visit coincided with a frontier autumn festivity which was gathering at New Haven Farm. The local populace apparently turned out in full force. Perhaps many of them came especially to meet the famous Virginia visitor. Although Washington did not mention this gathering within his journal, Crawford's daughter, Mrs. Margaret Crawford Styer, spoke of this event many years later. She recalled that while a fiddler played a series of merry tunes, Washington happily joined in the dancing. Throughout his life, he was well known as an adept, graceful dancer. He also demonstrated to spectators a celebrated ability to crack walnuts between his knuckles. Still an athletic man, Washington willingly participated in several sporting events.

He demurred, though, when a local strongman, John Stinson, challenged him to a wrestling match. Washington claimed that he had not wrestled in many years. But Stinson insinuated that the "Virginia gentleman did so because he was afraid of trying a fall." Upon joining the competition, he easily disposed of several opponents, including Stinson. The irate Washington threw Stinson with a hip roll "so hard that he was nearly killed, being obliged to keep [in] his bed for several days."

At dawn, on October 17, Washington's party departed on horseback for Fort Pitt. Due to a recent drought, the Youghiogheny's channel was too shallow for boat traffic. Among Washington's companions were Dr. Craik, Colonel Stephen, and the Crawford brothers. Throughout their journey, they rode along the eastern shore of the Youghiogheny and Monongahela Rivers. Ever the surveyor Washington noted within his journal that the distance between Stewart's Crossing and Fort Pitt was "43½ measured miles."

Upon spending three days in Pittsburgh Washington and seven companions climbed into a large canoe. Their original destination was the confluence with the Muskingum River. While in that locale Washington encountered a party of Delaware warriors led by Chief Pipe, an old adversary. Subsequently, he chose to survey additional uncharted country further down river. He also was planning to acquire some additional valuable real estate in the process. Accordingly, Washington did not return to Pittsburgh until the third week of November.

Following two days in Pittsburgh, on November 23, the travelers started out toward New Haven Farm. A heavy snowstorm, though, forced them to take shelter in a tavern at Turtle Creek. Moreover, two days later they found that the Youghiogheny water level was too high to ford on horseback across to Crawford's farm. And the high, fast water had caused the ferry boat to drift away. Washington recalled that after waiting for three hours "a canoe was got in which we passed and swam our horses."

Although some additional snowstorms made traveling difficult, on December 1, Washington finally reached Mount Vernon. Initially, he planned to undertake regular business tours. Within several years, however, he was involved deeply within the American Revolutionary War. He did not return to western Pennsylvania until 1784.

The Westsylvania Statehood Scheme

DURING THE period before the outbreak of the American Revolution, in April 1775, the thoughts of most British North Americans were concentrated upon the growing conflict with England. But the frontier residents of the Upper Ohio Valley were confronting another crisis. For several years the colonies of Pennsylvania and Virginia had presented rival sovereignty claims over this territory. By 1774, the dispute had intensified after Virginia officially incorporated the region within their newly created West Augusta District. Subsequently, the Virginia legislature sub-divided this district into three new counties, including one named Youghiogania

The initial sessions of the Youghiogania Quarterly Court were convened within the home of Andrew Heath which stood along the Monongahela River near the modern town of Floreffe in Allegheny County. Not surprisingly, most Pennsylvanians living near the Ohio River headwaters loudly denounced this annexation attempt. One group of locals, however, put forward their own solution to the controversy.

On June 18, 1776, a mass public meeting convened in Pittsburgh which was chaired by Captain David Rogers, a former member of the Virginia House of Burgess. The sovereignty issue was discussed thoroughly by the participants who rejected the competing claims of both Virginia and Pennsylvania. As an alternative, they proposed that the residents of the Upper Ohio River settlements should convene a series of conclaves soon. At these meetings, therefore, they were to select delegates for a convention at Becket's Fort. This stockade was within modern Forward Township in Allegheny County. This convention was supposed to establish a plan for creating a new state. Those delegates were to designate specific geographical boundaries, and form a provisional government. Those at Becket's Fort also would be electing two delegates to attend the Continental Congress in Philadelphia. They ultimately were to represent the new state "as the fourteenth link in the American Chain. "Apparently, the Becket's Fort Convention met during the third week of July.

Meanwhile, Rogers and his associates refused publicly in Pittsburgh to take the official loyalty oath to Virginia required of all white settlers living within the region. Furthermore, they wrote a petition addressed to the Continental Congress officially requesting immediate recognition of their proposed new state, By August, copies of this petition were circulating around the Pittsburgh area.

Within the petition, the authors stated that most of the local citizenry was disgusted with the ongoing territorial dispute. The petitioners blamed the trouble upon the intrigues of Virginia officials and a faction of land speculators from Pennsylvania. They pointed out that the capitals of both states were hundreds of miles from Pittsburgh. Accordingly, such distances made it impossible for either government to be responsive to the hundreds of families living beyond the Allegheny Mountains. A more logical solution, therefore, was the creation of the new state to be named Westsylvania.

The projected boundaries of Westsylvania included lands now within Virginia, Pennsylvania, West Virginia, and Maryland.

Furthermore, with the plan's success, Pennsylvania would have been separated from its southwestern corner encompassing the Youghiogheny and Monongahela River. The petition probably reached the Continental Congress during the autumn of 1776. Although the statehood plan initially was supported by several New England representatives the general congressional reaction was negative. Not surprisingly, the Virginia and Pennsylvania delegations, including such strong figures as Richard Henry Lee, George Mason, and James Wilson lobbied vigorously against Westsylvania. Their combined strength ensured that the petition would be buried within the congressional committee system. In fact, there is no evidence that Congress ever formally discussed the petition.

The resounding rejection of the petition by the Continental Congress effectively forestalled this statehood effort, thereby causing such agitation around Pittsburgh to cease for the moment. But some groups beyond the Allegheny Mountains periodically continued to call for separation. By 1780, though, many of these separatists had migrated down the Ohio River toward Kentucky. And David Rogers was killed during an Indian skirmish in Kentucky several years later. Virginia and Pennsylvania, moreover, made progress in settling the boundary dispute which became effective in May 1783.

River of the Falling Banks

WHEN BRITISH explorers began traveling into western portions of Virginia, they encountered a major river flowing northward beyond the Allegheny Mountains. The various Native American tribes were asked about their name for this waterway. Invariably, they were told it was known as the Monongahela, which literally meant "the river with the falling banks."

The Monongahela River is generally known to extend 290 miles in length. And the main channel which flows into western Pennsylvania is the culmination of two distinct feeder streams. The eastern extension is called the Tygart's Valley Branch and runs 118 miles before joining its western counterpart. The West Fork flows approximately 94 miles prior to the confluence which occurs within modern West Virginia. Consequently, the main course flows for 126 miles through both West Virginia and Pennsylvania, culminating at Pittsburgh.

Early European travelers noticed that the Monongahela was bordered directly by long stretches of hilly terrain, with some of these hills being 400 to 600 feet in height. At various points, these bluffs rise abruptly from the river channel. But other hills stood some distance behind the flat bottomlands directly fronting the river. Apparently, those hillsides frequently experienced major landslides. Moreover, they discovered that the river banks were subject to a high degree of steady erosion. Much of this was caused by channel blockages, including beaver dams and floating debris jams. Consequently, the contours of the alluvial plains constantly were changing, especially after flooding. They could agree with the Native American description of the Monongahela as "the river with the high banks which fall in." Subsequently, such erosion later was enhanced by white residents when artificial obstructions, especially wharves and dams, became common upon the Monongahela.

In 1753, George Washington initially saw the river and spelled it within his journal as the *Monongeyala*. The fur trader, Conrad Weiser, utilized the spelling of *Mohongaly* upon his various hand-drawn maps. A well-known early town resident, Hugh M. Brackenridge, wrote about the Monongahela in May 1786, within the Pittsburgh *Gazette*. He wrote: "The word Monongahela is said to mean in several Indian languages [to be] 'Falling in Banks.'"

Perhaps the best explanation was furnished, in 1775, by the Moravian missionary. John Heckwalder. He declared that the name was derived from two Delaware [Lenape] words "menonawan" and "hela." The first word literally meant "digging away banks," whereas the second could be translated as "running water." And he said the proper pronunciation was "Monangehella." Heckwalder placed the secondary accent on the second syllable and the primary emphasis upon the fourth. He also consistently provided the present spelling of Monongahela. All told, Heckwalder appears to have provided the final word on the subject.

A Matter of Jurisdiction

BY THE summer of 1770, British royal officials in London had resolved that Fort Pitt was no longer of strategic importance. Accordingly, the garrison troops were deployed to other North American outposts. But the abandoned fortress standing at the Ohio River's headwaters was of notable interest to the colonial governments of Pennsylvania and Virginia. Both colonies had been pushing competing claims to the frontier lands west of the Allegheny Mountains. Moreover, that rivalry persisted, in April 1775, after the outbreak of the American Revolutionary War.

On February 26, 1773, the Pennsylvania Colonial Assembly had established Westmoreland County, the twelfth, and the last county created during the colonial period. The establishment of Westmoreland was meant to enhance Pennsylvania's authority over the region. The initial county seat was Robert Hanna's settlement of Hannastown, situated upon the Forbes Road about 35 miles east of Pittsburgh. The Westmoreland Quarterly Court's first session, in April 1773, convened in Hannastown.

Meanwhile, Virginia's royal governor, John Murray, the Earl of Dunmore sourly noted these developments from Williamsburg, Virginia. A sizeable number of Virginians already were living around Pittsburgh. They claimed this region was part of West Augusta District, the most northern subdivision of Augusta County located within the distant Shenandoah Valley. By January 1774, Governor Dunmore had appointed John Connolly to be "Captain Commandant" of West Augusta District. Apparently, Connolly was known primarily for being George Croghan's nephew. Upon deciding to make Fort Pitt his headquarters, with a squad of armed Virginians, he occupied the stockade. He infuriated most local Pennsylvanians by renaming the old fortress as "Fort Dunmore."

By early 1775, everyone living beyond the Alleghenies had become aware that armed conflict between rebellious colonists and the British military was imminent in New England. On April 30, the news reached Pittsburgh that fighting was occurring around Boston, Massachusetts. Connolly promptly declared publicly his loyalty to George III, and the British Parliament. In essence, Connolly was an avowed Loyalist [Tory], working actively to arouse the local citizenry against the American Revolution.

On May 16, many American patriots assembled within a broad field nearby to the fort. They ultimately elected a Pittsburgh Committee of Public Safety, consisting of 38 members. Both Virginians and Pennsylvanians, temporarily forgetting the sovereignty issue, embraced the American cause. Connolly was dismayed to discover the local militia units no longer would be complying with his orders. Nevertheless, he remained in Pittsburgh for the next couple weeks.

From his Fort Pitt headquarters, he dispatched letters to known Loyalists living around the region. Moreover, he contacted various pro-British Native American chieftains within the Upper Ohio Valley. He reportedly urged them to attack those frontier settlers supporting the revolutionary cause, specifically noting that the Youghiogheny settlements were full of such sympathizers.

When Connolly's machinations became common knowledge, a Pennsylvania militia leader, Captain Arthur St. Clair of Ligonier, decided to act. On July 10, with an armed party, he arrested Connolly at his Pittsburgh home. Under heavy guard, the prisoner was slated to be sent eastward to Carlisle. With the aid of three confederates, however, he escaped captivity and fled, eventually reaching a British naval flotilla at Portsmouth, Virginia. He continued his correspondence with assorted Loyalists west of the Allegheny Mountains. Furthermore, he exhorted the Ohio Valley tribes to launch bloody forays against their American enemies.

Fully aware of Connolly's activities, the Virginia legislature authorized a Pittsburgh resident, Captain John Neville, to command a militia force and occupy Fort Pitt. After Connolly's departure, the fortress had regained its old name. Upon assembling at Winchester, Virginia, Neville's one-hundred troops marched northward along Braddock's Road. But many Pennsylvanians feared that their mission mainly was to ensure Virginia's rule over the Ohio River headwaters.

In response to this notion, several companies of Westmoreland County militia mustered at Hannastown. The overall commander of the 120 Westmoreland troops was Lieutenant Colonel Archibald Lochry, then living nearby to Chestnut Ridge. They quickly proceeded along the Forbes Road into Pittsburgh. Consequently, they were in town when their Virginia counterparts reached the scene.

After much discussion, on September 11, 1775, the two armed forces jointly occupied Fort Pitt. Not wishing to remain indefinitely in Pittsburgh, Lochry agreed that Neville should be Fort Pitt's commandant. Revolving militia units from both states subsequently served as garrison troops. Neville remained in charge at Fort Pitt for fourteen months. During this interlude,

Neville spent a great deal of time renovating the long-neglected fortifications, and bolstering the available arsenal. Neville was unable, though, to forestall a series of Anglo-Indian frontier on his watch.

By January 1777, the Continental Congress finally decided to assume direct responsibility for the strategic bastion. Upon General George Washington's recommendation, Brigadier General Edward Hand was appointed as the new commandant. With a force of Continental Army regulars, Hand arrived in Pittsburgh during the last week of May. Accordingly, on June 1, 1777, Neville formally ceded command to Hand. A new period in Fort Pitt's history had begun. Aware that a bounty had been placed upon him, John Connolly wisely never returned to western Pennsylvania.

A Most Valuable Commodity

MID THE American Revolutionary War, the
residents along the Youghiogheny River would
have noticed a variety of small vessels carrying
full sacks heading downriver toward Pittsburgh. Upon reaching
their destination the boats docked along the Monongahela River
Wharf. Within a couple of days the contents of those sacks had
been poured into kegs and stored upon larger flatboats, bound
for New Orleans, Louisiana Territory, then under Spanish rule.

Quite often those goods were used by traders to barter for
shipments of gunpowder, which were vital for the American
war effort. They resorted to such transactions, due to the lack
of legitimate coinage throughout North America. Actually,
the Americans' most valuable export commodity was flour.
Furthermore, flour production was the initial commercial
industry to develop within western Pennsylvania.

With the outbreak of hostilities, Spanish officials governing
the Louisiana Territory quietly had reversed a policy of placing
severe restrictions upon receiving trade goods from British
North America. Although officially neutral in the conflict, they
tacitly were supporting the American revolutionaries. With
the assistance of resident American merchants, notably Oliver
Pollack, flatboats containing flour cargoes were arriving from

western Pennsylvania. The region virtually had become the "breadbasket" for the region beyond the Allegheny Mountains. There apparently was a great demand for flour within the lower Mississippi Valley. Both the Youghiogheny and Monongahela Rivers possessed bottom lands containing rich topsoils. Accordingly, settlers had established farms that cultivated various crops, including wheat and corn.

Upon being harvested the wheat husks were taken to the nearest mill where meal, free from the bran, was ground into fine powder. Subsequently, the flour was placed either in sacks or kegs. These goods were destined for transportation along the river within a variety of boats. Meanwhile, much of the corn crop was distilled into whiskey. Many boatmen often augmented their flour cargoes with a few kegs of corn whiskey. By all accounts, the local shippers began their annual sojourns in late February, providing the rivers were not frozen over. The hauling season usually lasted until June. But some traders were known to undertake their junkets in November.

These were the periods when the channels possessed water levels of sufficient depths to accommodate boat traffic. The smaller boats usually contained several sacks, while a flatboat could carry a much heavier load. A common practice was for many boats to rendezvous at McKee's Point [McKeesport} near the junction of the Youghiogheny and Monongahela. The bulk of the produce, moreover, would be placed in the largest flatboats. Those vessels proceeded in flotilla toward the Monongahela Wharf in Pittsburgh. On April 28, 1782, Brigadier General William Irvine, the Fort Pitt commandant, wrote that already he had issued trading permits to the owners of ten flatboats containing flour cargoes. He also estimated that 3000 tons of flour would be heading down the Ohio River from Pittsburgh that year.

Each vessel generally required a crew of five men. Within a span of fifteen months approximately fifty flatboats ultimately docked in New Orleans. They apparently possessed an aggregate cargo of 5000 flour kegs originating from western Pennsylvania. While heading down the Ohio River the shippers usually made stopovers at several settlements along the southern shore in Kentucky. The northern bank in Ohio commonly was regarded as enemy territory.

The British and their Indian allies often attempted to intercept those trade vessels. River lore had it that the area within the vicinity of the Scioto River's mouth particularly was dangerous. On the Kentucky side was a tall rock formation known as the "Watch Tower." From this vantage point, enemy lookouts watched for approaching flatboats. A favorite ploy was for a white man, usually a Tory [Loyalist] renegade to appear on shore begging for assistance. Claiming to have escaped from Native American captivity, he pleaded to be taken on board. In any case, when the unwary crew stopped to render assistance Indian warriors promptly attacked. Several American sojourners, therefore, lost their lives at the Watch Tower. Consequently, most savvy traders passed that dangerous spot at night.

A notable figure within the flour trade was Jacob Yoder, a German migrant who had settled in Lancaster County. By 1780, he had traversed the Glades Road within the vicinity of Jacobs Creek near the Youghiogheny. In late April 1782, Yoder had departed downriver from Pittsburgh with a flatboat full of flour, and grain. A major customer of Yoder's was Gaspard Markle who owned a sizeable flour mill near the mouth of Big Sewickley Creek. Upon reaching the Watch Tower, Yoder purportedly recognized the so-called "captive" to be Simon Girty, a notorious renegade. Years earlier the two men had met several times at Stewart's Crossing when they were trapping along the

Youghiogheny. Of course, Yoder told his crew to keep moving. While proceeding down the Mississippi he made stopovers, to sell his various goods in St. Louis and Natchez. On June 5, he finally pulled into New Orleans.

While in that city he booked passage upon a schooner bound for Havana, Cuba. He already had sold his cargo and boat for a tidy profit. He also had acquired from Oliver Pollack a consignment of deer hides and fur pelts. Once in Havana, he sold off those good to European traders. Subsequently, aboard an American sloop, Yoder reached Baltimore. He apparently undertook similar trading junkets for many years. By 1798, though, Yoder had relocated permanently to Maysville, Kentucky.

Two French nationals, Bartholomew Tardineau and Jacques de Honore, in 1782 made a similar voyage originating on the Monongahela River at Redstone [Brownsville], bound for New Orleans. Upon reaching Fort Henry [Wheeling} they decided to divide their cargo, and proceed within two separate flatboats. At the Watch Tower, they managed to drive off Indian attackers in canoes. These two enterprising Frenchmen also reached New Orleans safely. They remained active in the river trade for a couple more years.

Not surprisingly, the garrisons of various American outposts along the Ohio River were good customers. For instance, at any given time 4000 flour casks could be found within the warehouse of Fort Nelson [Louisville] in Kentucky. The traders were seeking to lighten their loads to navigate the treacherous "Falls of the Ohio" several miles downstream from Fort Nelson. That flour later was sold locally.

After the American Revolutionary War concluded in 1783, the need for Spanish gunpowder slackened. The Spanish authorities, moreover, resumed their policy of imposing severe restrictions upon American traders operating along the lower Mississippi River. Meanwhile, new American settlements, including Marietta, Ohio, were being established throughout the Ohio River Valley. With the increasing amount of wheat growing locally, there was no need to import flour from western Pennsylvania. Other important commodities, notably coal, became far more important. By 1800, the exporting of flour had ceased to be a vital economic endeavor around Pittsburgh.

A Most Deadly Mission

MID THE final months of 1777, reports were reaching Pittsburgh that a formidable force of Canadian rangers and their Native American allies from western New York would be mounting an invasion down the Allegheny River. And other Indian raiders already had been undertaking raids from Ohio. Unfortunately, though, the local militia units lacked the necessary military supplies, notably gunpowder. Several Virginia expatriates, therefore, sought aid by writing Governor Patrick Henry in distant Williamsburg. To solve this problem Henry looked to Captain David Rogers of Redstone, a Monongahela River settlement. Some years earlier the two men had served together within the Virginia legislature.

Initially, Henry was reluctant to intervene since Virginia and Pennsylvania both claimed ownership of the region surrounding the Ohio River's headwaters. He knew that Pennsylvania partisans would be highly critical of his intervention. Nonetheless, he felt that it was vital to purchase a large store of gunpowder from Spanish colonial authorities in Louisiana Territory. This was the closest available source for such procurement in North America. Many observers probably noted Henry's choice of Rogers to lead this mission. A native of Henrico County, Rogers had relocated to the "Monongahela Country" in 1768. He settled originally at Stewart's Crossing upon the Youghiogheny River. He subsequently was William Crawford's partner in several business ventures.

Throughout the next several years Rogers also purchased land tracts along both the Youghiogheny and Monongahela Rivers. By 1772, he had settled permanently upon a farm nearby to the confluence of the Monongahela and Redstone Creek. Although once a Virginia legislator, Rogers did not support actively that state's claim to the region. Instead, in 1775, he became a leader of a movement to create a new state of Westsylvania. On June 26, a large public meeting convened in Pittsburgh which was presided over by Rogers. They dispatched two delegates to the Continental Congress in Philadelphia with a mass petition requesting that statehood be recognized for Westsylvania. Not surprisingly, both the Pennsylvania and Virginia congressional delegations effectively forestalled this effort.

Rogers subsequently supported the cause of "independency" during the American Revolutionary War. Governor Henry evidently chose him largely upon the recommendation of Major General Adam Stephen who was in Williamsburg at the time. He probably pointed out that Rogers already was familiar with the Ohio River, due to earlier trading junkets. By April 1778, Rogers was ready to begin his important mission. He had assembled a detachment of forty men at Colonel William Crawford's plantation of New Haven Farm.

They rode northward to Pittsburgh, where two large flatboats were purchased. Prior to departing they filled those boats with a cargo of flour. Among Rogers's crew was Basil Brown, a member of the family which founded Brownsville, a major Monongahela River town. By May 20, the expedition departed Pittsburgh and within six weeks had reached the Mississippi River. At the river town of Natchez, Rogers informed Spanish officials about the reason for his visit. The Spaniards confirmed that a sizeable amount of gunpowder was stored within a supply depot at St. Louis. The military commandant, however, added that the necessary sales documents had to be obtained in New Orleans. Accordingly, Rogers and several companions headed down river.

The return trip up the Ohio was uneventful until they reached the mouth of Licking Creek [Kentucky] upon the river's southern bank. Because the northern shore in Ohio commonly was regarded as hostile "Indian Country," the sojourners made camp upon the Kentucky side. But the British and their Indian allies were aware of Rogers's mission. Consequently, Native American spies had been monitoring their progress for many days. An Anglo-Indian war party, therefore, decided to stage an ambush at Licking Creek.

At dawn, on October 10, one of Rogers's sentries spotted a small group of Shawnee braves crossing over the Ohio into Kentucky, seemingly unaware of the Americans' presence. Not suspecting they were decoys, Rogers made the fateful decision to attack, unaware that formidable force was waiting in ambush within the surrounding forest. Accordingly, the attack caught the Americans completely by surprise, with only thirteen of them ultimately surviving the resulting massacre. One survivor later reported that most of the enemy warriors either were Shawnee or Miami. By all accounts, Rogers received a fatal tomahawk wound early in the fight. Despite a diligent search two months later his remains were never found. Some observers subsequently surmised that the corpse had been devoured by wolves.

Meanwhile, his chief deputy, John Knotts successfully escaped by dodging into the nearby forest. Several weeks later after he reached the safety of Fort Pitt, word of the massacre circulated throughout the region. Although another survivor, Robert Denham, had escaped the carnage by scaling a tall tree, severe wounds in each leg prevented him from walking away. Upon shooting a raccoon he heard someone approaching through the brush. He was relieved to discover Basil Brown who was shot in the right arm, and the left shoulder. With both arms useless he kicked the dead "critter" toward an open fire. Throughout the next couple weeks, Brown successfully drove similar small game toward Benham, waiting nearby with a loaded musket. The two men remained at that locale for more than a fortnight.

On several occasions they observed Native American hunters walking along the opposite shore. A passing flatboat finally rescued the pair and transported them down the river to Fort Nelson [Louisville], Kentucky. In any case, the enemy had conveyed all the gunpowder to Fort Detroit. The two empty flatboats already had been found floating aimlessly in the Ohio River. Basil Brown eventually returned to his farm nearby to Redstone Creek. Interestingly, Benham relocated to Kentucky after the war, establishing a farm nearby to the town of Newport. He essentially resided about five miles from the massacre site. Benham probably recalled the horrific episode every time when passing that spot.

George Rogers Clark at Big Sewickley Creek

IN MARCH 1781, General George Rogers Clark had traveled northward from Virginia into western Pennsylvania along Braddock's Road. With the full backing of George Washington, he was intending to raise a force of 2000 troops beyond the Allegheny Mountains. Three years had passed since Clark's noteworthy expedition into the Northwest Territory. He was aware, though, that Americans living upon the frontier were facing much danger because of the depredations of the British and their western Indian allies. Clark believed that this problem could be solved by capturing the various British bastions on the Great Lakes, notably Fort Detroit.

After arriving within the region, however, he was dismayed that many Pennsylvanians were not supportive of his proposed campaign. For instance, he discovered that only a small number of Westmoreland County militia would be gathering at a proposed muster on Big Sewickley Creek, a Youghiogheny tributary. Many residents were Pennsylvania loyalists and suspected that he had ulterior motives. They believed he was planning this expedition to further enhance Virginia's sovereignty claim over the Upper Ohio Valley.

Throughout the autumn of 1780, Clark's various military aides already had traveled throughout the region. They had experienced some success procuring flour and livestock. But these agents had scant luck in persuading local male residents to enlist with the expedition. This problem was the case around Big Sewickley Creek., especially among native Pennsylvanians. For instance, Colonel Christopher Hays of the Westmoreland County militia vocally argued against Clark. He predicted that Clark's expedition would be a definite military fiasco. Furthermore, Clark's primary aim was to assure Virginia rule throughout the Northwest Territory.

By March 12, Rogers had arrived in western Pennsylvania. Initially, he made his headquarters at New Haven Farm, Colonel William Crawford's home upon the Youghiogheny. Crawford advised him to emphasize that his primary mission was the subjugation of the main Ohio Indian tribes, especially the Shawnee, Delaware, and Wyandot. Those pro-British tribes were a more tangible threat to the region than Fort Detroit. The notion of punishing them, therefore, would be quite popular among frontier residents. Apparently, this change of emphasis had a favorable effect around Big Sewickley Creek.

In late May, Colonel Hays summoned Westmoreland militia officers to a meeting at Captain John McClelland's farmhouse. During this conclave, on June 18, Hays reiterated his opinion that Rogers was being deceitful about his ultimate military goals. He also stated that the Fort Pitt commandant, Colonel Daniel Brodhead, shared his suspicions about Clark. To Cox's disgust, though, most of the militia officers voted to contribute three hundred troops. At that point, a furious Cox rode back to his home in Hannastown, the county seat. After his departure, Colonel Archibald Lochry was chosen to command the Westmoreland contingent,

Subsequently, Lochry rode to New Haven Farm and conferred with Clark. They agreed the muster should occur, on July 16, at Big Sewickley Creek, within a field nearby to Gaspard Markle's grist mill. The historian, Edgar W. Hassler, stated this date was chosen "to enable the farmers' to finish their wheat and harvesting before taking down their rifles and powder horns."

A couple of days prior to the muster Clark and Lochry, on horseback rode to Big Sewickley Creek. To their dismay, however, this event failed to occur on schedule, Colonel Hays and his allies had persuaded many of these "citizen soldiers" to remain home. Moreover, reports were circulating that Colonel Brodhead was refusing to allow any Continental Army troops to participate within the expedition. Another disappointment was that various farmers were refusing to supply Clark's force with adequate quantities of either food or livestock.

While Lochry remained behind to salvage the situation, Clark headed down the Youghiogheny River within a skiff toward the junction with the Monongahela. After gaining some recruits in that locale he traveled onward to Fort Pitt. At that point, he engaged in a nasty confrontation with Brodhead, who steadfastly refused to place any of his troops under Clark's command. Accordingly, Clark decided to make his local headquarters down the Ohio River at the mouth of Chartiers Creek. But only a modest number of additional troops arrived at this encampment.

Another major problem was that during mid-summer the Ohio's main channel often became too shallow for adequate navigation. Clark was forced, therefore, to march his soldiers overland toward Fort Henry [Wheeling], Virginia. He was aware that Indian spies were monitoring his every move. Moreover, during the march, several groups of recruits deserted. He was pleased, however, that following some heavy rainfall the river's water level had risen. After a brief stopover, on August 8, within a fleet of flatboats Clark's force proceeded down river to Fort Nelson [Louisville], Kentucky.

During his stay at Fort Nelson Rogers realized that his campaign was in deep trouble. Approximately three hundred able-bodied men remained in camp, an insufficient number to mount an effort against Fort Detroit. Furthermore, there was no word that significant reinforcements were on the way. And he knew his provisions were running critically low. A final problem was that winter was approaching rapidly. Upon reviewing the situation with his staff, on October 5, Rogers reluctantly agreed to call off the expedition. Consequently, most of his command departed in small groups to their homes either in Virginia or Pennsylvania. By early November a bitter George Rogers Clark was in Pittsburgh, where he blamed publicly various local leaders, notably Brodhead and Hays, for his abortive campaign.

Meanwhile, Clark also garnered some concrete details about a tragic episode. Following Clark's departure from Big Sewickley Creek Colonel Lochay successfully assembled a force of Westmoreland County militia. By August 8, Lochay and one hundred riflemen were encamped at Big Sewickley Creek. They were planning to march overland along the Glades Trail toward Fort Henry. But they reached that destination several hours after Clark's departure. While following him down the Ohio, Lochry's command subsequently experienced a devastating attack far down the river not far from Fort Nelson. During that bloody ambush most of them, including Lochry, were killed.

Colonel Crawford's Gruesome Death

B Y THE spring of 1782, Colonel William Crawford was living in quiet retirement at New Haven Farm near Stewart's Crossing upon the Youghiogheny River, two years after resigning his Continental Army commission. In May 1782, however, his old friend General George Washington urgently requested that he return to active duty, and lead a force of volunteer militia troops against the Native American tribes living in Ohio. But Crawford was ambivalent about assuming this new command. After completing his legal will, on May 16, he began his westward journey.

He was not impressed when he initially saw the five hundred frontier troops encamped at Mingo Creek [Steubenville, Ohio]. Some critical onlookers, including George Rogers Clark, already regarded them as an undisciplined rabble. As they began the march, on May 25, Crawford's men were in good spirits. Unfortunately, though, they quickly wasted their food rations and ranged through the forest wasting ammunition while shooting at game. Breaking camp each morning invariably was a slow process. And the column frequently halted to await a myriad of stragglers.

They spent four days following an Indian trail to the Tuscarawas River. One hundred miles further was their main target, a large Wyandot village at Upper Sandusky. Not surprisingly, Indian scouts continually had been observing their progress. Fully aware of Crawford's military objective, therefore, a formidable Anglo-Indian force was preparing an ambush nearby the village. Assorted parties of Wyandot, Shawnee, and Delaware warriors were congregating in Upper Sandusky. Furthermore, a large contingent of Canadian rangers, under Captain William Caldwell, had arrived from Fort Detroit. By June 8, Crawford's troops had reached the vicinity of Upper Sandusky within modern Wyandot County, Ohio. Due to many desertions, this force already was depleted seriously.

Within two days the enemy completely had encircled the column, and wiped out the supply train. After a day of hard fighting, Crawford realized he was facing superior firepower. A scout reported, moreover, that the enemy steadily was gaining reinforcements. They already had inflicted heavy casualties upon the Americans. Accordingly, that evening Crawford ordered his men to attempt a breakout southward to the Ohio River. Although portions of them successfully escaped, Crawford and several companions were captured by Delaware warriors.

They subsequently were marched off to the Upper Sandusky stronghold. Upon reaching that destination most of the captives summarily were executed by the victors. At Upper Sandusky, a leading Delaware chieftain, Captain Pipe, physically attacked Crawford, a longtime personal enemy. With much fanfare, Captain Pipe painted Crawford's face black, the mark of death. Consequently, Crawford was removed to a nearby encampment at Tyrnochtee Creek. The only other captive with him was an army surgeon, Dr. John Knight.

The victorious captors began celebrating with heavy drinking which got them into a homicidal mood. But Crawford saw a onetime friend, Simon Girty, who had been serving the British since March 1778. Prior to the American Revolutionary

War, Girty was a familiar figure around the Youghiogheny River Valley, both as a fur trapper and Indian scout. He had visited New Haven Farm on several occasions. Despite their earlier association, however, Girty refused to intervene on Crawford's behalf. He made no attempt to stop the systematic torture of him. An impassive Girty watched as his Delaware allies finally burned Crawford at the stake. Crawford's ghastly ordeal apparently took place over several hours.

Meanwhile, Knight was led off to Captain Pipe's lodge a couple of miles away. While passing by Knight discerned Crawford's charred remains within the fire pit. Although several warriors wanted to kill Knight, Captain Pipe refused their demands. The Delaware chieftain also told Knight that he bore him no animosity. Accordingly, with Captain Pipe's likely connivance the physician later made his escape. And no one made any serious effort to recapture him. After wandering for several weeks, on July 24, Knight finally reached Pittsburgh. He confirmed to horrified residents the rumors about Crawford's grisly death. Furthermore, George Washington expressed great sadness upon receiving those grim tidings. But this episode has a sequel.

In 1845, Henry Blackstone, the future general superintendent of the Pittsburgh and Connellsville Railroad, was in Zanesville, Ohio on business. As Blackstone traveled toward Connellsville on horseback along the National Road, he made a stopover at a roadside inn. At this point, he noticed that an elderly Native American man was watching him from a nearby bench. During their subsequent conversation, the old man said he was among the last of the Wyandot tribe still living in the area.

When Blackstone said that he was from the Youghiogheny Valley, the Wyandot said that region was familiar to him. As a youth, he had often traveled along the Youghiogheny River. He also remembered Colonel Crawford "the big white chief from the Youghiogheny," and witnessed his actual execution in 1782. And he recalled passing that grim spot many times over the years. The elderly man also said the "Great Spirit" had not "let grass grow where the white chief burnt." There never had been any vegetation upon that site except some hard, dry moss. With that revelation, the two men parted company. Upon reaching home, therefore, Blackstone had an interesting tale to tell his Connellsville neighbors.

George Washington's Unpleasant Western Tour

DURING THE summer months of 1784, George Washington was feeling restless at Mount Vernon. He had returned permanently to his estate the previous December. Over the next seven months, he had worked hard to stabilize his plantation's financial situation. After eight years of commanding the Continental Army amid the recent war, however, he found that peacetime was tedious. Furthermore, since 1770 he had not visited his extensive properties beyond the Allegheny Mountains. For nearly four decades the general had purchased large land tracts throughout the region. Accordingly, on September 1, 1784, he departed Mount Vernon on horseback, bound for a western tour of two months. Accompanying him were his lifelong friend, Doctor James Craik and an anonymous African American male slave.

Within four days the sojourners had reached Warm Springs, Virginia, a village at the eastern slope of the Alleghenies, where two younger men joined the party. They were the general's nephew, Bushrod Washington, and Craik's eldest son, William. Subsequently, the five men rode northward over the Allegheny Plateau into western Pennsylvania. They traversed Braddock's Road, a route that Washington had surveyed three decades earlier.

By September 10, they were lodging at the Red House Tavern, adjacent to the old campsite of General Braddock's army. The following morning, they passed through Great Meadows toward the confluence of the Youghiogheny and Casselman Rivers.

Interestingly, Washington chose not to reminisce with the others about his French and Indian War exploits within that locale. Instead, he talked about the economic potential of his several hundred acres located nearby. He was gratified that the tenants on his Great Meadows farm were producing a good grain crop that year. And he declared that a successful inn could be established locally upon another strategic parcel facing Braddock's Road.

Much of Washington's western Pennsylvania real estate had been selected by his former land agent, Colonel William Crawford of New Haven Farm [Connellsville]. Prior to the American Revolution Crawford had purchased for his client many choice tracts upon the Youghiogheny. He also had ensured that all subsequent tenants paid their rents on schedule. But Crawford's violent death, on June 11, 1782, at the hands of hostile Native American warriors out in Ohio, dramatically changed the situation for Washington.

With some trepidation, on September 13, Washington reached Washington's Bottom {Perryopolis], where most of the residents lived upon his real property. He owned approximately 1500 acres around that village. His primary investment, though, was a grist mill which he never had seen. He promptly noted the edifice, consisting of three stories, was in acute physical disrepair. Moreover, the mill race virtually was dry, and clogged with debris. A furious General Washington publicly upbraided the manager, Gilbert Simpson, for gross incompetence. He also ordered Simpson to vacate a nearby farm that he had been renting.

Washington's mood was not improved by the sudden appearance of some unexpected visitors. They were a delegation of residents from Miller's Run, a settlement several miles southwest of Pittsburgh. Most of them were Scots-Irish migrants living upon land parcels claimed by Washington since 1767. Unfortunately, though, the legal documents proving Washington's ownership apparently had been lost since Crawford's untimely passing. Those "squatters" had assumed, therefore, that they were the lawful owners of their farms. Not surprisingly, their subsequent interview with Washington became rancorous. The general was discovering that many westerners were not in awe of his illustrious reputation east of the mountains.

That evening Washington decided to sell the improvident gristmill at public auction. He also intended to sell off the farm which Simpson was renting. At 10:00 A.M., on September 15, Washington arrived at the mill to start the bidding. Initially, he was encouraged that a large crowd was in attendance. The historian, Joel Achenbach, has written that the general soon realized "that the people had come not to buy . . . but rather to gawk." They viewed this affair as an excellent bit of public entertainment. Much to Washington's chagrin, no one responded positively to three separate bid calls. After twenty minutes of abject futility, he abruptly terminated this debacle.

Meanwhile, he also had scant luck in selling off the farm, because Gilbert Simpson was a popular local figure. After some contentious bargaining Washington grudgingly agreed that Simpson could remain upon the property. Rather than paying his annual rent in cash, though, Simpson was to forward five hundred bushels of wheat to Thomas Freeman, Washington's new local agent. Before departing the area, on September 16, Washington personally collected overdue rents from a score of obdurate tenants. Furthermore, he forced several other renters to sign new lease agreements. Most observers agreed that the general was a tough landlord. Bushrod Washington later noted that his uncle was aware of "every schilling he was due, every acre he owned." Accordingly, most residents probably were relieved to watch his departure.

The travelers proceeded along the Youghiogheny for about ten miles. They eventually rode cross country through Rostraver Township in Westmoreland County, toward the Monongahela River. They eventually crossed the river at Devore's Ferry [Forward Township]. Upon crossing the Monongahela they entered Washington County which the Pennsylvania General Assembly had created three years earlier. Subsequently, Washington made a series of stopovers to inspect assorted real properties within this county. He invariably became embroiled in a series of noisy confrontations with the various alleged squatters upon those tracts. In marked contrast, however, the sojourners were greeted warmly when reaching Pittsburgh.

Washington initially had intended to extend his tour by traveling down the Ohio River. He wanted to review his respective land claims within the Upper Ohio Valley. Moreover, he wished to survey a desirable locale to construct the terminus for a proposed canal. For many years he had been interested in constructing an artificial waterway connecting the Potomac and Ohio Rivers. But reports were reaching Pittsburgh that hostile Miami warriors were aware of his travel plans. Somehow details about his itinerary had become common knowledge throughout the region. Consequently, a plan to ambush Washington's party was in the works. Heeding the warnings of his various Pittsburgh friends, he prudently canceled this final junket.

On September 21, the general and his companions made a brief return to Washington's Bottom, which proved uneventful. Washington ultimately sold the gristmill to Israel Shreve in 1795. He commenced heading southward along the Braddock's Road toward Virginia. His final Pennsylvania stopover was in Beeson's Town [Uniontown]. He was back at Mount Vernon by the second week of October. He had concluded a western tour which was eventful, and frustrating. And this was George Washington's final personal journey to the region surrounding Pittsburgh.

General Putnam Comes to Simeral's Ferry

WITH THE approach of 1788 within Westmoreland County, residents were anticipating the annual influx of migrants heading toward the western frontier. For nearly a decade the Glades Road had been utilized heavily by those seeking a fresh start in the Ohio Territory. This roadway extended westward from Bedford, Pennsylvania to the vicinity of Simeral's Ferry [West Newton] upon the Youghiogheny River. Many sojourners apparently preferred this route to the Forbes Road which ran some miles to the north. In early January reports were circulating that a notable American Revolutionary War figure, Brigadier General Rufus Putnam, was leading a party of forty-seven New Englanders, bound for the Upper Ohio Valley to establish a settlement. By February 2, he had reached his Youghiogheny destination.

A native of Sutton, Massachusetts, Putnam was born in 1738. While a teenager he began working as a surveyor around New England. During the French and Indian War, he had aided in constructing various British military fortifications around Lake Champlain. After the war he pursued a career as a mill right, thereby constructing many mills throughout the region.

He was hired, moreover, to survey major frontier grants within northern New England, and New York.

With the American Revolution's outbreak, in April 1775, Putnam commanded a militia company that joined the Continental Army's siege of Boston. During the next several months he established a friendship with the commander-in-chief, George Washington. In March 1776, Putnam was instrumental in constructing fortifications upon Dorchester Heights, overlooking downtown Boston. American artillery, therefore, was capable of inflicting heavy damage upon key British fortifications. Accordingly, on March 17, a force of 9000 British regular troops boarded a ship armada heading for Halifax, Nova Scotia. For his valuable service, Putnam was promoted to lieutenant colonel.

During the next several years, Putnam served with the Continental Army in the northern states. He helped design the West Point fortifications, the primary American stronghold upon the Hudson River above New York City. Subsequently, he was promoted to the rank of brigadier general. In June 1783, he formally retired from active military duty. In recognition of his capable service, the Continental Congress provided him with a large land grant in the Northwest Territory.

While living in Rutland, Massachusetts, Putnam joined with several other Continental Army officers from New England, to form the Ohio Company. He became president of this enterprise which sought to promote settlement within the Ohio River Valley. They planned to establish the town of Adelphia, adjacent to the confluence of the Muskingum and Ohio Rivers. Downriver from Wheeling, Virginia, Adelphia was meant to be the first major settlement within the Northwest Territory. And the new community would be built on acreage once claimed by George Washington. Most of the original Ohio Company members were army veterans from either Massachusetts or Connecticut. They pursued this endeavor aware that hostile

Native American war parties still ranged throughout the region. But Putnam was confident that Adelphia would be a commercial success.

By late January 1788, Putnam was leading a convoy of wagons and packhorses along the Glades Road, bound for Simeral's Ferry. His party was the vanguard for other settler parties intending to settle at Adelphia. All forty-seven men had accompanied from Massachusetts. They were greeted warmly by the ferry owner, John Simeral, who was among the earliest settlers in that part of Westmoreland County. At that locale, a small hamlet had formed known as Simeral's Ferry. He also was the proprietor of the local inn.

Upon encamping at Simeral's Ferry, Putnam reviewed his options regarding the remainder of the journey. Initially, he had planned to cross the Youghiogheny aboard the ferry and follow a wagon road toward the Monongahela. Apparently, their intention was to reach Elizabeth Town [Elizabeth Boro] and procure some flatboats traveling along that river. Putnam already had heard reports that a boatyard was being created in that town. In a few years, Elizabeth Town would become a major boat building center within the Monongahela River Valley.

Simeral and his associates apparently began pointing out the drawbacks to that plan. They warned that large feral hogs were roaming throughout the woods across the river. Those animals had grown notably huge from feasting upon acorns and chestnuts which were plentiful in that vicinity. And those beasts were dangerous to travelers, especially after nightfall. The residents of Simeral's Ferry were attempting to establish their own boat works. A large amount of lumber was available locally, notably around Big Sewickley Creek. With that plentiful lumber source wooden flatboats easily could be constructed.

Such river craft were oblong in shape, and flat bottomed. They were built on land, bottom side up, while the planks were attached to the gunwale with wooden pins. All calking also was completed while the boats were on shore. Upon being overturned within the water that boats' upper portions were completed. Movement with the river currents was aided by great oars rowed by burly occupants. These vessels already were known popularly as "Kentucky Boats." Putnam decided to remain at Simeral's Ferry to construct two flatboats, and forty-foot galley that he named the *Mayflower*. That vessel was to be powered by a set of canvas sails.

Accordingly, Putnam's party stayed upon the Youghiogheny for nearly two months. By March 20, their Kentucky Boats were ready for the voyage. Those vessels proceeded down the Youghiogheny, bound for Pittsburgh. By nightfall they had reached McKeesport, a way stop at the junction with the Monongahela River. With little difficulty, they reached Pittsburgh by late afternoon the following day. The galley followed in their wake a couple of days later. Upon securing their supplies the flotilla began heading down the Ohio River.

By April 7, the migrants had reached their destination at the confluence of the Ohio and Muskingum Rivers. Subsequently, they began the task of erecting the new town's first building. Throughout the next three years, additional settler parties kept arriving. Most of them also traversed the Glades Trail in the Youghiogheny at the Simeral's Ferry. But many of these migrants headed westward overland to Wheeling. At Putnam's suggestion, the town name was changed to Marietta. Not surprisingly, Marietta became an important commercial center in the Ohio Valley.

Meanwhile, General Putnam also achieved notable success out west. In 1790, President George Washington appointed him the Northwest Territory's first territorial judge. Six years later Washington also nominated him to be the first Surveyor General of the United States. Being a staunch partisan of the Federalist

Party, he was a political foe of Thomas Jefferson, the leader of the rival Democratic-Republicans Consequently, for overtly political considerations President Jefferson removed him from that post in 1808.

General Putnam, however, remained active within Ohio state politics for many years. On May 28, 1824, following a brief illness, Putnam died in Marietta. Perhaps during those final years, he fondly recalled those months on the Youghiogheny at Simeral's Ferry.

The Unpredictable Captain Pipe

THROUGHOUT THE summer of 1794, President George Washington was awaiting official news about the progress of an army, commanded by Major General Anthony Wayne, campaigning within the Northwest Territory. Two earlier expeditions against hostile Native American tribes had been military disasters. During this interlude, moreover, he received tidings that Captain Pipe, once a prominent Delaware [Lenape] leader had died near Marietta, Ohio. Washington probably was ambivalent about his passing, because he never had found him predictable.

By all accounts Captain Pipe was born, around 1725, at the Delaware village of Kittanning upon the Allegheny River. A scion of the Wolf Clan his Indian name was Wobocan. As an adult, he gained his nickname due to a penchant for smoking a corncob pipe. By 1750, he had become a tribal war chieftain. Although pro-British, initially he was not involved in the French and Indian War. In the fall of 1758, though, Captain Pipe led a Delaware scouting party during the westward march of Brigadier General John Forbes through the Allegheny Mountains toward Fort Duquesne. Amid this campaign he became acquainted with Colonel George Washington, then a young Virginia militia officer.

By the end of the war in 1763, Captain Pipe was not happy with the British. He was angry that numerous white settlers were moving on to lands within the Upper Ohio Valley claimed by the Delaware. Accordingly, he led a Delaware faction into an alliance of western tribes led by Pontiac, the charismatic Ottawa chieftain. During the first week of August 1763, Captain Pipe participated in the Battle of Bushy Run. Due to superior firepower, the British troops under Colonel Henry Bouquet eventually won the battle. Several hours later one of Bouquet's patrols apprehended Captain Pipe. He was imprisoned at Fort Pitt for the next six months. Always a persuasive talker he ultimately convinced Bouquet that he was no longer a threat.

After his release, the chieftain resided at his tribal village of Coshocton in Ohio. In late October 1770, George Washington traveled down the Ohio River on a surveying expedition. Accompanying him was his primary land agent, Captain William Crawford. At the confluence of the Ohio and Muskingum Rivers, they encountered Captain Pipe. There is no indication that this meeting was hostile.

With the outbreak of the American Revolutionary War, in April 1775, Captain Pipe aligned with the British. Despite his strong opposition, however, the Delaware decided to remain neutral during the early years. But reports were circulating that some of Captain Pipe's followers had been with Shawnee war parties on forays into western Pennsylvania. Furthermore, he was known to be in touch with notorious Loyalist leaders, Simon Girty, and Alexander McKee. Assuming that the Delaware now were hostile, the Americans committed several unprovoked attacks against them. On April 20, 1779, Colonel Daniel Brodhead, the Fort Pitt commandant, led a punitive strike against Coshocton.

They shot down a score of warriors, burned the village, and drove off the livestock. Most survivors relocated to Captain Pipe's new stronghold at Upper Sandusky. Consequently, Delaware warriors now were active openly in raiding missions against the American settlements. In May 1782, another American army commanded by Colonel William Crawford began an abortive campaign against Upper Sandusky. Unfortunately, though, Indian spies had been watching Crawford's column from the outset.

By June 12, a superior Anglo-Indian force had encircled the American troops. Amidst a desperate breakout effort, many Americans, including Crawford, were taken prisoner. Captain Pipe was excited that Crawford was among the captives. He evidently held him responsible for the deaths of several close friends. He personally painted Crawford's face black, indicating imminent death. Following several hours of physical torture, Crawford was burned alive at Tynoochee Creek, about a mile from Captain Pipe's lodge. Apparently, the Delaware chief never expressed any remorse for his role in the execution.

Nevertheless, within a year he dramatically reversed his attitude about the Americans. In June 1783, the Continental Congress designated a peace envoy, Colonel Ephraim Douglass, to ride westward from Fort Pitt into Ohio. He was to inform the western tribes that the war was over. In any case, Douglass received a warm welcome from Captain Pipe at Upper Sandusky. Douglass later recalled that his host now regarded the British as "false friends." He repeated that sentiment at several inter-tribal councils.

Throughout the post-war years, Captain Pipe consistently advocated friendship with the United States. During the autumn of 1784, George Washington was in western Pennsylvania on personal business. And it was common knowledge that he planned to make a canoe trip from Pittsburgh to the Scioto River. But Captain Pipe told some white traders that Miami warriors were plotting an ambush. His warning reached Pittsburgh, thereby prompting Washington to cancel that trip.

He also was within the vicinity when General Rufus Putnam and his New England migrants arrived at the junction of the Ohio and Muskingum Rivers in 1788. Accordingly, he watched as they founded Marietta, the first permanent town within Ohio. A prominent visitor, Colonel John May of Boston, in his journal, on August 2, 1788, remarked that Putnam had introduced him to "Old Pipes." The elderly Delaware leader often ventured into Marietta on trading junkets.

By 1793, the aging Captain Pipe was in failing health. He played no role in the efforts of Little Turtle, the Miami chieftain, to organize the western tribes against the United States. Little Turtle was enraged that American migrants were settling throughout the Northwest Territory. Whether Captain Pipe opposed Little Turtle's cause is unknown. The old man spent his last years in a village about forty miles from Marietta. In May 1794, he died of natural causes in his lodge. Three months later, on August 8, 1794, General Anthony Wayne's troops inflicted a decisive victory over Little Turtle's forces at the Battle of Fallen Timbers.

Recalling Nicholas J. Roosevelt

WESTERN PENNSYLVANIANS are familiar with the Roosevelt family of New York. Two of the greatest American presidents were Theodore and Franklin Delano Roosevelt. They both traveled through the region during their lifetimes. The latter's wife, Eleanor Roosevelt, also made several visits to western Pennsylvania as the first lady. The initial member of that family to become well-known beyond the Allegheny Mountains was their distant relative, Nicholas James Roosevelt. During the spring of 1811, he gained fame in Pittsburgh for introducing the first working steamboat into the Upper Ohio Valley.

By all accounts, he was born, on December 27, 1767, in New York City, the son of Isaac and Anne Roosevelt. His father was a banker, and an overseas commercial merchant. He had invested in a series of lucrative trading voyages to East Asia, notably China. Isaac Roosevelt also held several municipal offices in New York City. But Nicholas never showed any interest in following his father's example. From an early age, he displayed an aptitude for mathematics and mechanics. While spending one summer on an uncle's farm he built a small mechanical boat, propelled by paddle wheels mounted on both sides. And he created a set of small springs, made either from hickory wood or whalebones, circulating upon an unwound cord wrapped around wheel axles. Accordingly, this small boat moved around his uncle's mill pond at three miles per hour.

By 1793, he had become the manager of the New Jersey Copper Mine Association. The company was attempting to reopen a copper mine on the Passaic River near Arlington, New Jersey. Following eighteen months on the job, Roosevelt suddenly quit. At that point, his interest in industrial steam power was paramount. He was corresponding with James Watt, the Scottish inventor of the modern steam engine. Watt provided him with much good advice about steam engine manufacture. Roosevelt also imported two of Watt's engines from Great Britain.

Meanwhile, he had purchased a land tract upon Second River near Belleville, New Jersey. Upon the property, Roosevelt constructed both a foundry and machine shop which he called the Soho Works. He subsequently added a copper rolling mill to fulfill a large order for the United States Navy. With the full approval of President John Adams, Secretary of Navy Benjamin Stoddert, in 1798, commissioned him with a major project. He was expected to supply rolled copper for the construction of six new frigates in Philadelphia. To fulfill his contract by an April 1801 deadline, Roosevelt was obliged to spend much of his financial capital.

Unfortunately, though, in the presidential election of 1800, Adams was defeated by Thomas Jefferson. Upon taking office, in March 1801, President Jefferson reviewed Roosevelt's contract. Regarding major naval construction as an example of wasteful government spending, he decided to void the project. Jefferson apparently was indifferent that this cancellation would cause severe financial hardship for Roosevelt. Within a few years, Roosevelt's fiscal problems forced the closing of Soho Works.

One pleasant event occurred, on November 15, 1806, when Roosevelt married Lydia Latrobe in Philadelphia. The bride's father was Benjamin Henry Latrobe, Sr. the famous architect. The two men had become friends while Roosevelt was working on a steam-powered vessel. He had been hired by Robert Livingston and John Stevens to build this craft. The new steamboat, the *Polacca*, on October 20, 1798, made a successful short trip upon the Schuylkill River. As a precaution, Roosevelt had maintained a steady speed of five miles per hour. But Livingston was critical of Roosevelt's decision to place paddle wheels on both sides of the boat. This dispute was unresolved, in May 1803, when Livingston accepted President Jefferson's appointment as U.S. Minister to France. Within two years Livingston and James Monroe had negotiated the Louisiana Purchase Treaty.

Amid the extensive negotiations. Livingston had become interested in the trade potential of the Mississippi River Basin. He also had met Robert Fulton, another enterprising American seeking to build a steamboat. Interestingly, Fulton's proposed craft included Roosevelt's concept of vertical paddles. With Livingston's financial backing, in 1807, Fulton's steamboat, the *Claremont*, completed a roundtrip voyage on the Hudson River between New York City and Albany. Accordingly, the Livingston and Fulton Steamboat Company soon had a thriving business around eastern New York. And these partners were intent upon creating a presence in North America's inland rivers.

Through Latrobe's good offices, in 1809, they hired "Nick" Roosevelt to supervise the building of a wooden steamboat in Pittsburgh. Before construction commenced, however, within a keelboat Roosevelt ranged both the Ohio and Mississippi Rivers to acquire useful navigational knowledge. He also gained additional information from all the veteran boatmen to be found around the Monongahela Wharf. Roosevelt's genial personality made him a popular figure around town. He eventually built the *New Orleans*, which was seventy feet in length and possessed vertical paddle wheels. The steam engine was placed within the hull below the boat's single deck. Initially, he completed several test runs up the Monongahela River toward McKeesport.

A sizeable crowd gathered at the Monongahela Wharf, in April 1811, to watch the *New Orleans* depart down the Ohio, bound for Louisiana. Despite numerous natural obstructions, Roosevelt somehow managed to make his destination within six weeks. Although the steamboat remained in New Orleans Roosevelt boarded a schooner heading to New York City. Upon returning home Roosevelt sought a full partnership in the Livingston and Fulton Steamship Company. Neither senior partner, however, was willing to grant this demand. But Roosevelt was more successful, on December 1, 1814, in securing a federal patent for his vertical paddle innovation.

By 1830, Roosevelt had retired from all activities involved with steamboat construction. Instead, he became devoted to developing his extensive landholdings in western New York. With his wife, he resided on a large farm in Onondaga County, New York. But he continued to follow all the major technological innovations occurring within the United States. After a short illness, on July 30, 1854, Nicholas James Roosevelt, passed away at home. For the record, "Nick" also was President Theodore Roosevelt's great grand- uncle.

The Legend of Johnny Appleseed

MOST WESTERN Pennsylvania residents probably do not recognize the name of John Chapman. But they do know him by his popular nickname, "Johnny Appleseed." Chapman essentially is known for wandering throughout the frontier territories of the Old Northwest planting apple trees in numerous locales. Few readers, though, are aware that he often procured his valuable seed from within Westmoreland County.

By all accounts, John Chapman was born near Boston, Massachusetts, in 1775. He later loved to tell friends that his family lived a short distance from Breed's Hill, which on June 17, 1775, became the site of the famous American Revolutionary War battle. During Chapman's early childhood, however, his family relocated to Springfield, Massachusetts. As a youth, he developed the habit of wandering over the New England countryside studying all manner of wild plants. Decades before Henry David Thoreau, he knew all about the botanical life around Walden Pond. Throughout his life, he possessed an encyclopedic knowledge regarding North America's natural resources. Apparently, at an early age, he developed a special interest in the apple.

By 1795, Chapman somehow had made his way into western Pennsylvania. He spoke later about his familiarity with the courses of both the Youghiogheny and Monongahela Rivers. Furthermore, he ranged up the Allegheny River into western New York. Various commentators have agreed that Chapman, in 1800, was living within a small shack in the Pittsburgh area. For several months Chapman visited the many cider presses operating regionally, especially in Westmoreland County. Within the vicinity of Three Mile Creek, a Monongahela tributary above Pittsburgh, he built an unusual river craft, consisting of two canoes lashed together. And he stored as cargo several barrels of rotten apples. With little fanfare, in April 1800, he headed down the Ohio River toward Steubenville, Ohio.

He consistently claimed that his first apple orchard was planted within a meadow two miles down-river from Steubenville. He created a second grove further south at Licking Creek. Contrary to popular myth, Chapman did not scatter seeds in a random manner. He carefully created an orchard network which was visited annually for maintenance. For many years Chapman routinely returned to western Pennsylvania for his seed supply. By 1810, Chapman had made his base of operations within Ashland County, Ohio. During the winter months, he resided upon a farm owned by his sister's family near Mansfield. With the coming of spring, he began walking hundreds of miles to inspect his respective orchards.

Customers often bought an apple sapling from him for a penny. Chapman, though, was known to accept in exchange either old clothes or a hot meal. Moreover, he readily extolled for free to prospective buyers about the wide variety of products which could be derived from an apple tree. Even by frontier standards, Johnny Appleseed wore outlandish attire. While clad in ragged trousers, his upper garment was an old coffee sack, with holes cut out for his arms and head. He also liked to wear a battered pan for a hat. Amid the warm months, he preferred to walk barefoot. But some eyewitness later swore that Chapman periodically wore conventional clothing when it suited him.

The Native American tribes within the Northwest Territory possessed great admiration for Chapman, believing him to be a medical healer of the highest order. He was known to favor such herbal remedies as catnip and pennyroyal. Unlike most of Chapman's white peers, he exhibited great kindness toward all animals, wild and domestic. He argued that all manner of species held unique, valuable niches within the natural order.

Although an undeniable eccentric, Chapman was not a simple illiterate man. A good botanist, he was familiar with a diverse range of horticultural issues. And various observers were surprised that Johnny Appleseed was well-versed in biblical questions. Apparently, he adhered especially to the religious tenants of Emmanuel Swedenborg, a Swedish theologian. At an outdoor revival in Indiana [circa 1830] a Baptist preacher had asked rhetorically, "Where is the man . . . like the primitive Christian, who walks about . . . barefoot and in sackcloth." Standing under a nearby tree Chapman loudly declaimed, "Here is that primitive Christian!"

By 1820, Johnny Appleseed had planted orchards in Ohio, Kentucky, and Tennessee. Every year he made the rounds inspecting those trees. Amid the next decade, moreover, Chapman established a new base of operations near Fort Wayne, Indiana. Accordingly, he created new orchards within Illinois, and Michigan.

During the autumn of 1846, the aging Chapman went to Zanesville, Ohio, reportedly to inspect an orchard severely damaged during a severe thunderstorm. While returning to Indiana he evidently suffered a bout of bronchitis. Within a few days that illness had evolved into pneumonia. Chapman's once robust constitution apparently could not withstand this ailment. Consequently, he sought refuge at the farm of an old friend,

William Worth, in Allen County, Indiana. After spending several weeks under the care of the Worth family, on March 11, 1847, he passed away in his sleep. Chapman's remains were interred within a nearby Fort Wayne cemetery.

Although Chapman was gone physically, his myriad of apple trees outlived him by many years. And descendants of those trees still survive within many locales into the 21st Century. Accordingly, readers may consider the tangible gift that John Chapman bequeathed to the United States.

Memories of Isaac Meason

WHILE DRIVING down Route 119 in Fayette County about seven miles northeast of Uniontown, motorists are likely to notice an imposing stone house. This building once was the residence of Isaac Meason, a Virginia expatriate, who lived there in the early 19th Century. Although Meason chose to call his home Mount Braddock, that name had not originated with him. Furthermore, he was not the original owner of that property. The noted frontier explorer, Christopher Gist, initially had claimed that land around 1750. Upon this landholding, he established the first English settlement west of the Allegheny Mountains.

Gist was in residence, in June 1755, when Major General Edward Braddock's army passed by during his unsuccessful effort to capture Fort Duquesne. Following their decisive defeat, on July 9, the remnants of this army sought refuge at Gist's settlement. When vengeful French-Indian war parties began raiding the area, Gist and his fellow settlers fled into Virginia. After the French and Indian War, though, Gist chose not to return to the region.

Nonetheless, his eldest son, Thomas Gist [circa 1765], resettled upon the property, which stood at the foot of Chestnut Ridge's western slope. His farm also was adjacent to Braddock's

Road, the primary northern route out of Virginia. Thomas Gist apparently began calling his "plantation" Mount Braddock. On October 12, 1770, George Washington and his traveling companions made a brief stopover at Gist's place. Washington later wrote in his journal that Mount Braddock "lay low," and possessed soil "as rich and black as possibly could be." Washington did not return to the region until 1784. During this second trip Gist provided Washington's party with a noonday meal. At that point, another Virginian Isaac Meason already had settled upon a farm not far from Gist's place.

Meason was born, in June 1743, in Henrico County, Virginia He eventually followed Braddock's Road through the Allegheny Mountains into western Pennsylvania around 1770. Within a few years, he had purchased 300 acres from Thomas Gist. In addition to farming, he reportedly held several local public offices prior to the American Revolution. With the outbreak of the American Revolutionary War, in April 1775, Meason supported "independency" from Great Britain. He served as a captain in a company of Westmoreland County militia, then the official local jurisdiction. For the remainder of his life, he often was referred to as Captain Meason.

On April 28, 1778, Thomas Gist, the local magistrate officiated over the marriage of Isaac Meason and Catherine Harrison of Winchester, Virginia. For some reason, though, the couple chose not to announce publicly their marriage for many months. This union ultimately produced two sons and a daughter.

In October 1779, Westmoreland County voters elected Meason to be their representative to the Pennsylvania legislature. By 1783, he was elevated to the Supreme Executive Council of Pennsylvania. He also was an advocate that Pennsylvania ratify the new Federal Constitution in 1787. At that point, Meason retired permanently as an active politician, preferring to concentrate upon business concerns.

Apparently, by 1790, Thomas Gist was deceased and Meason had bought most of his landholdings. In fact, Meason already had acquired extensive acreage throughout western Pennsylvania. But he was not content to remain a farmer, and a land speculator. He was aware that the late Colonel William Crawford of New Haven Farm [Connellsville] in 1781 had been intending to mine a "bank of iron ore" upon some lands he owned located along the Youghiogheny River. In June 1782, however, Crawford had been killed by enemy warriors at Upper Sandusky, Ohio. Within a few years, therefore, Meason had bought that property and began extracting the iron ore. Since that locale possessed additional iron deposits, he sought to establish an iron smelting operation.

Meason organized a partnership with Morton Dillon and John Gibson in 1791. Subsequently, they established Union Furnace, the first successful ironworks beyond the Allegheny Mountains. A couple of years later Gibson left the business. Subsequently, Meason, Dillon and Company built a larger foundry, which observers said featured the finest blast furnace in North America. They produced a variety of useful products, including, stoves, pots, kettles, and skillets. They were providing the necessary commodities for the thousands of migrants heading into the Ohio River Valley. Their business was located approximately fifteen miles east of Brownsville, a major town upon the Monongahela River. During the next decade, Meason had created several other smaller furnaces around the region.

By 1798, Meason was in Great Britain surveying the burgeoning British iron and steel industry. And he particularly was intent on studying their techniques in constructing iron bridges. Consequently, he hired an English architect, Adam Wilson, to build comparable structures in western Pennsylvania. During the next several years, Meason's architect had erected three iron spans along the Youghiogheny. The most notable crossed the river at Connellsville. Further north a second bridge spanned Jacob's Creek. The third bridge spanned Big Sewickley Creek not far from West Newton.

Meanwhile, Meason devised a second task for his English architect. By 1800, Wilson had designed for him a spacious mansion made primarily from limestone. Meason's house is the only seven-part residential structure ever built within the United States. As the architectural historian Franklin Tokar has written, "The Meason house is not only the most important early house in western Pennsylvania but also one of the most significant . . . dating from the early republic anywhere in the country." Meason's dwelling was meant to resemble the stately colonial plantation houses of his native Virginia. And he revived the name of Mount Braddock for his new home.

Over the years, Meason had purchased 30,000 acres of real estate in Pennsylvania, Ohio, and Kentucky. Many of these tracts contained valuable mineral deposits, especially coal and iron. Among numerous other investments was a lucrative salt works in Bedford County. By 1810, he was among the wealthiest men in Pennsylvania. Two years later Meason agreed to meet with Thomas C. Lewis, a recent Welsh immigrant. Lewis wanted to establish a mill designed specifically for rolling wrought iron into solid bars, a process he had learned in Wales. Nevertheless, no major ironmaster was interested in helping him.

But Meason quickly discerned the potential in financially backing Lewis's proposed enterprise. In 1816, the partners erected Ross Furnace which stood northwest of Ligonier in Fairfield Township, Westmoreland County. This new industrial plant was an important step within the development of the iron and steel industry in western Pennsylvania. Interestingly, Ross Furnace remains standing in 2017.

Meason entered this last great investment as his health was declining. Accordingly, he was not involved in managing Ross

Furnace He already had turned over his diverse business interests to his sons. He passed away quietly, on January 20, 1819, at Mount Braddock. This stately mansion remains a tangible reminder of Isaac Meason's once formidable presence in western Pennsylvania affairs.

Washington and Gist meet Queen Aliquippa

Sir William Johnson

Chief Pontiac

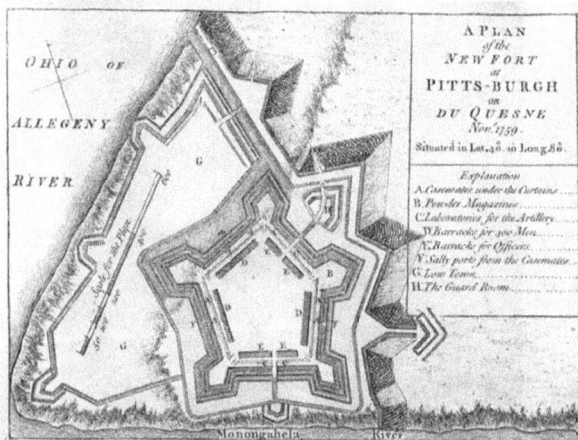

Fort Pitt

Fort Duquesne

Christopher Gist

Young George Washington

Colonel William Crawford

The death of General Braddock

General Rufus Putman

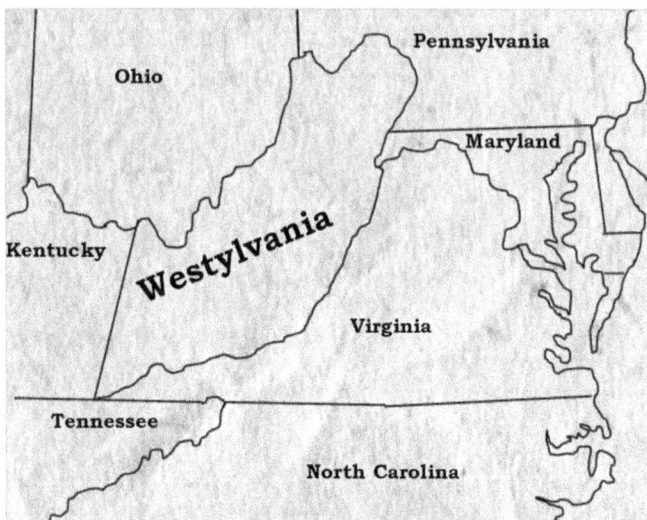

The potential state of Westsylvania

John Heckwalder

George Rogers Clark

Nicholas Roosevelt

Edward Hand

Steamer New Orleans *replica in Wheeling harbor, 1911*

Isaac Meason house

Johnny Appleseed

Henry Miller Shreve

Stephen Foster

Sydney Rigdon

Henry Clay Frick

Edgar Cowan

Andrew Carnegie

General James A. Ekin

A Real River Man

BY JULY 1795, George Washington had owned a grist mill in Washington's Bottom [Perryopolis] in Fayette County for nearly three decades. Despite the high expectations, however, that enterprise never had proven lucrative. Consequently, he had been trying to sell that mill for years. Washington, therefore, was pleased to learn that Colonel Israel Shreve was interested in acquiring the mill. Shreve had moved to Fayette County a year earlier and intended to reside in Washington's Bottom with his family. His young son, Henry Miller Shreve, was destined to be a notable national figure.

By all accounts, Henry Miller Shreve was born, on October 23, 1785, in Babington County, New Jersey. Although a Quaker, his father had served as an officer in the Continental Army during the American Revolution. When Henry was a small child the family moved to Cumberland, Maryland. After buying some land in Fayette County, Colonel Shreve learned that the grist mill was for sale. Although various locals warned him otherwise, Shreve made the purchase in 1795. Within five years, though, the colonel had died from heart disease. The mill was productive enough for Henry Shreve to transport grain cargoes by barge down the Youghiogheny River to the confluence with the Monongahela at McKeesport. There he joined a convoy of "grain boats" heading to Pittsburgh.

Subsequently, he began a freighting business, which conveyed diverse merchandise to Pittsburgh, thereby becoming a familiar figure at the Monongahela Wharf. He was proficient in handling Kentucky boats, keelboats, and pirogues. He ranged along the various local rivers within those different vessels. Meanwhile, his mother, Mary Cokeley Shreve, had sold the grist mill, prior to moving to Connellsville with a new husband. By 1807, Shreve was using a Kentucky boat to convey fur consignments between Marietta, Ohio and St, Louis. And he also was making regular keelboat runs between St. Louis and Pittsburgh.

Shreve began to traverse the Mississippi River's upper reaches. For instance, he conveyed a lead cargo [circa 1810] from Galena, Illinois to New Orleans. Upon marrying Mary Blair, in June 1881, Shreve settled in Brownsville, Pennsylvania, then a thriving boat construction center along the Monongahela. And he became a full partner in a local boatyard.

Amidst a junket to Louisville Shreve learned that Robert Fulton's *New Orleans* had become the first steamboat operating on the Mississippi. Consequently, Shreve and his partners constructed the *Enterprise*, a stern-wheeler eighty feet in length. In December 1814, Shreve took this vessel from Pittsburgh to New Orleans with a cargo full of military supplies for Major General Andrew Jackson's army. Several weeks after his arrival Jackson dispatched Shreve and his boat into the Gulf of Mexico to exchange prisoners with the British fleet. In May 1815, the *Enterprise* reportedly was the first steamboat to travel along both the Ohio and Mississippi Rivers to Louisville.

Following this achievement, Shreve was in Wheeling to supervise the construction of a new steamboat, the *Washington*. Unlike his earlier vessels, this one possessed a flat, hollow hull, and a high-pressure engine mounted on the main deck. Furthermore, the *Washington* was the initial steamboat to feature a second deck. Unfortunately, though, a gasket burst within the main cylinder, therefore, causing the earliest western steamboat explosion, resulting in several deaths. Undaunted, however, Shreve designed several new vessels modeled upon the *Washington*. By 1819, Shreve's steam packet, the *Post Boy*, was conveying mail regularly to various towns along the western rivers.

As his western operations expanded, though, he came into direct conflict with the powerful Fulton and Livingston Steamship Company. Through their congressional allies, including U.S. House Speaker Henry Clay, they had been granted monopoly rights over all steam navigation within the Louisiana Territory's inland waterways. Accordingly, they initiated major litigation against Shreve. But ultimately Shreve won the case in federal court. All comparable steamboat companies, therefore, would be operating freely within the Mississippi River Basin.

Meanwhile, President John Quincy Adams, in January 1827, appointed Shreve to be Federal Superintendent of Western River Improvements. Within a couple of years, Shreve personally had designed the first "steam snag boat." This singular craft was meant to remove the myriad of sunken tree trunks which clogged many river channels. Such hidden obstacles previously had constituted a primary menace to river navigation. Observers began calling Shreve's handiwork "Uncle Sam's Tooth Pullers." Those snag boats apparently broke loose the logs, and dragged them on board. Subsequently, this fractured wood became the fuel that enabled the boats to continue operating.

By 1837, Shreve's boats managed to break up completely the notorious "Red River Raft," an obstruction that had existed for centuries. This natural barrier essentially had forestalled successful economic development throughout northwest Louisiana. While undertaking that endeavor, Shreve had purchased several sizeable land tracts around the Red River. Consequently, he had designed a small town near Bennett's Bluff in Louisiana. That village, by 1839, had grown sufficiently to be incorporated as Shreveport. Shreve remained in office throughout the Democratic presidential administrations of Andrew Jackson and Martin Van Buren. He formally retired from that position in April 1841.

Due to various successful business ventures, Shreve was secure financially during his final years. With the death of his first wife in 1828, he later had married Lydia Rogers of Cairo, Illinois. The couple resided upon a plantation near St. Louis, Missouri. Surrounded by his family, on March 6, 1851, Henry Miller Shreve died at home. When hearing of his passing assorted older Youghiogheny River Valley probably recalled his early days hauling grain on that waterway.

A High-Quality Coal

MID THE middle years of the 19th Century, coal mining had become a major industry within western Pennsylvania. Throughout the region, miners were extracting that vital fuel commodity from rich veins of bituminous [soft] coal. But a century ago another popular name for this product was "Youghiogheny Coal." By 1850, numerous coal mines were operating along the Youghiogheny River Valley from Connellsville to McKeesport.

Coal mining already had been occurring within that region for more than a century. For instance, in October 1770, Colonel William Crawford had shown George Washington a coal mine nearby to Stewart's Crossing [Connellsville]. Within his daily journal, Washington noted that coal was plentiful and "of the very best kind, burning clearly . . ." A later local historian, George H. Thurston, wrote in 1860: "Throughout the whole extent [Youghiogheny Valley] the finest bituminous coal is easily mined, and in the lower markets of the Ohio and Mississippi Rivers 'Yough Coal' . . . is [of] the leading quality."

Thurston added that all through the Ohio River Valley consumers commonly regarded this coal to be of "peculiar excellence." Consequently, this high-grade product commanded a better place upon the open market, notably east of the Mississippi

River. All the Youghiogheny mines initially dispatched their coal consignments down the river by barge toward Pittsburgh. From that point, this fuel cargo was conveyed throughout the Ohio Valley. And shipments of "Yough Coal" were known to reach the Mississippi River communities below St. Louis, Missouri.

Nonetheless, that setup was altered permanently in the late 1850s when the Pittsburgh and Connellsville Railroad began regular operations. Railroad corporations eventually became major consumers, and the primary conveyors of the coal mined upon the Youghiogheny. Given the high grade of coal being mined locally, coke producing enterprises soon began appearing within the Youghiogheny Valley, especially between Connellsville and West Newton.

Not surprisingly, Yough coal assured that the coke produced within those early beehive ovens was of the highest quality. By 1846, the primary coke operation at Broad Ford, owned by A. S. M. Morgan, reportedly was producing 1000 bushels per day. Morgan's coke apparently was shipped to customers as far west as Indianapolis, Indiana. The site of these works ultimately was purchased by Henry Clay Frick in 1872.

But much of the purported Youghiogheny Coal was not produced along that river at all. A greater quantity originated in mines upon the Monongahela River. Moreover, by 1880, various Youghiogheny enterprises already were ceasing operations. But the old trade name persisted while the river shipments to the Ohio and Mississippi ports continued flourishing. Coal dealers simply preferred using that familiar label when advertising any cargoes from western Pennsylvania. All shipments from the Monongahela Valley were sold the "Yough" brand.

When making price quoted to "first pool coal' these dealers utilized that familiar name to draw customers. As the historian, Richard T. Wiley, once remarked: "Coal in immense quantities was sold under the Youghiogheny name which was never nearer that stream than to pass its mouth [at McKeesport] if it was mined higher up along the Monongahela." By 1910, this trade largely had run its course. There were fewer sizeable coal loads being drawn from mines along the Youghiogheny. Accordingly, most current readers have no knowledge that "Youghiogheny Coal" formerly possessed such an illustrious reputation.

Composing Along the Monongahela

A PERSISTENT TRADITION has existed in South Carolina that Stephen Collins Foster, the famous American composer, about 1850, paid a visit to a plantation upon the Pee Dee River. Furthermore, he became so enamored with the river's natural beauty that the composer wanted to use the name in the lyrics of an upcoming song, "The Old Folks at Home." But the New York publishing house, Firth, Pond and Company substituted the name Swanee name into the text. There are two problems with this story. Foster never visited South Carolina during his lifetime. And he personally had chosen that name, in 1851, while sitting within an office upon the Monongahela Wharf in Pittsburgh, the composer's hometown. He made the selection while gazing upon the Monongahela River

Contrary to another story, Foster did not travel widely through the southern states. During the late 1840s, he spent fourteen months working in a river freighting firm owned by his elder brother, Dunning Foster, in Cincinnati, Ohio. While living there he often crossed over the river into Kentucky. He also was prone to walk about the wharves listening to the African American laborers singing their songs while unloading boat cargoes. Two of his popular songs, "Camptown Races" and

"Ring, Ring de Banjo," reflect the black dialect he heard during such strolls. He was known to follow the same routine when living in Pittsburgh.

Upon returning to Pittsburgh, Foster surprised everyone by marrying Jane Denny McDowell, on July 22, 1850. Nonetheless, the young couple waited two years before taking a belated honeymoon. On February 20, 1852, the Fosters and several companions embarked upon a steam packet, *James Millinger*, bound for New Orleans, Louisiana. The couple apparently undertook no significant side excursions, amid the voyage, and their New Orleans stay. Consequently, the only parts of the "Sunny South" that Foster ever saw were the lands adjoining the Mississippi and Ohio Rivers. At that point, he was awaiting the release of "The Old Folks at Home" by the publishers.

The main reason that southern themes were common in his music was due to financial necessity. Foster often wrote "plantation melodies" for the various minstrel show companies. During their shows, the performers wore black makeup and sang songs emulating an African American dialect. Accordingly, "The Old Folks at Home" was typical of this genre. Within his sketchbook, Foster initially had written in the song's opening line, "Way down on the old plantation." But he soon changed the wording to "Way down upon the Pedee ribber." Subsequently, he recalled that this South Carolina waterway already had been used in a minstrel show. Some anonymous composer had written "Ole Pee Dee" in 1844.

Although this song melody did not resemble his own tune, Foster decided that the name was shopworn. At that point, he decided to consult with his brother, Morrison Foster, the chief clerk of a commercial shipping firm, which had an office on the Monongahela Wharf. From Pittsburgh's earliest days this part of town was known as the "Mon Wharf." As was his habit, the composer entered his brother's office without notice. He promptly asked, "What is a good name of two syllables for a southern river." He spurned his brother's initial suggestions of Pee Dee and Yazoo.

Accordingly, Morrison produced a comprehensive marine atlas map that included all the inland streams of North America. After studying the relevant maps, the brothers noted the Suwanee River in northern Florida, hardly a notable waterway. Upon pondering the name for several minutes, the composer began humming his proposed tune. He then declared, "Yes, that's the one." Without further comment, he walked outside abruptly and began pacing along the wharf. He always became oblivious to his surroundings when contemplating a proposed song. Knowing his brother's crotchets, Morrison did not give the matter a second thought. Meanwhile, within his sketchbook, he later wrote, "Way down the Swanee River." The publishers chose to entitle the song as, "The Old Folks at Home." Whatever the name, the song became a big hit.

By 1850, Stephen Foster had moved to New York City to pursue a career as a full-time professional composer. His marriage virtually had disintegrated several years earlier in Pittsburgh. Among his many songs produced in this period, only "Beautiful Dreamer" proved noteworthy. Along with experiencing dire poverty, he was also a chronic alcoholic. After being severely injured in a fall in his rooming house, on January 16, 1864, he died at Bellevue Hospital. Upon examining his personal items, hospital workers found a brown leather purse containing thirty-eight pennies. Approximately one penny for every year of his life.

There also was an envelope upon which he had written in pencil, "Dear friends and gentle hearts." Morrison Foster later suggested that these words were the title for a new song. Although a prolific composer, Foster had declined writing many songs reflecting distinctive western Pennsylvania themes. He never mentioned any local rivers, including the Monongahela, within his lyrics. While pacing along the Monongahela Wharf, however, he formulated the final touches of one of his most popular tunes, "The Old Folks at Home."

He Hauled the Coal by Barge

A FAMILIAR SIGHT along the western Pennsylvania rivers are the motorized towboats pushing coal barges along their channels. This writer has observed that practice countless times within the vicinity of the U.S. Steel Clairton Coke Works on the Monongahela River. Those barges usually are docked a short distance upstream at West Elizabeth. And the towboats often push several barges simultaneously. That practice, however, was unknown until William H. Brown, a shrewd entrepreneur, conceived the idea in 1855.

William Henry Brown was born, on January 15, 1815, in North Huntingdon Township, within Westmoreland County, Pennsylvania. His parents, James and Sarah Brown, had relocated there from Carlisle, Pennsylvania several years earlier. His education consisted of the subjects taught him at the local common grammar school. As a teenager, he worked on the family farm during the summer. Amid the colder months, he earned money by digging soft coal [bituminous] from a small mine located upon an uncle's farm situated along the Youghiogheny River. Subsequently, he sold this coal to various neighbors for fuel to heat their homes during cold weather. He learned, therefore, that many western Pennsylvanians preferred purchasing coal rather than digging it for themselves at some nearby mine.

Brown initially made purchase deals with several Youghiogheny coal operators. He also bought a horse and wagon to haul coal to customers around North Huntingdon Township. Brown eventually was covering a much wider territory, and owned a wagon fleet. He had hired several teamsters to make those deliveries for him.

By 1845, Brown began to float coal barges down both the Youghiogheny and Monongahela Rivers toward Pittsburgh. He sold his coal consignments to customers along the Monongahela Wharf on a regular basis. Furthermore, he purchased his own coal mine along Pigeon Creek, nearby to Monongahela City in Washington County. He also became a full partner in the Kensington Iron Works in Pittsburgh. Through Brown's business connections the company bought a coal mine up the Monongahela at Nine Mile Run's mouth. He also built a local riverside depot to sell coal to passing steamboats.

Apparently, in 1855, Brown conceived the idea of utilizing small steam vessels, known as towboats, to push coal barges down the Ohio River beyond Pittsburgh. The prevailing practice of floating barges was both problematic and costly. Consequently, the hauling costs regularly exceeded the profits in such ventures. By 1855, Brown conceived a much better plan. He purchased twelve barges capable of holding 250,000 coal bushels. Those craft were placed in the water six abreast within two rows. These barges were lashed firmly together with iron cables. Two towboats, the *Scampas* and the *General Larimer*, were positioned behind the back barges.

Despite widespread skepticism, Brown announced that this flotilla would be traveling from Pittsburgh to Louisville, Kentucky. His eldest son, Samuel Brown, went along to make sure this consignment reached Louisville on schedule. The experiment helped establish the long-term success of the western Pennsylvania coal industry. By 1858, Brown was the primary stockholder of the Ross, Brown and Berger Coal Company. They soon purchased a major iron rolling mill in New Castle, Pennsylvania. Brown assured the purchase transaction by issuing a personal check of $100,000.

At the outbreak of the Civil War, in April 1865, Brown procured a lucrative contract to supply coal to the Federal military forces operating throughout the Mississippi River Valley. He established major coal depots at strategic river towns, notably Cairo, Illinois and St. Charles, Missouri. At this point, he owned a fleet of steamboats of various kinds. He held a series of discussions about the coal situation with President Abraham Lincoln, and Secretary of War Edwin Stanton. Prior to the war, Stanton had been on legal retainer with Brown's company. During this period Brown became good friends with General Ulysses S. Grant.

Throughout these years Brown often entered the war zones to supervise coal shipments. He was aware that Confederate officials had placed a cash bounty on his head, dead or alive. In fact, on one occasion a party of mounted guerilla raiders almost captured him. While standing on the main deck of a steamboat he once came under enemy sniper fire. After the war, Brown boasted that no coal shipment was ever hijacked by the Confederates. Moreover, nearly every delivery arrived on schedule.

By 1870, Brown owned twenty steamboats that traversed all the major internal waterways within the Mississippi Basin. Although physically robust throughout most of his life, chronic overwork eventually took its toll. Consequently, in April 1873, a major paralytic stroke forced him to retire. On October 12, 1872, he passed away at the Kirkbride Asylum in Philadelphia. News of his passing was met with sadness out in his native western Pennsylvania.

Finding Some Strange Objects

AMONG THE more prosperous residents within Fayette County, in 1859, was Colonel Alexander W. Hill. Although mainly known for his coke works, he was notable for another reason. Hill owned a farm where strange objects kept turning up, especially when his fields were plowed. A Mexican War veteran, Colonel Hill owned considerable real property upon the Youghiogheny River's western bank, approximately eight miles below Connellsville. At his cookery [coke works] stood rows of beehive ovens which produced 1200 bushels per day. He owned, moreover, a large salt well that reached a depth of a thousand feet.

The colonel liked to declare that, at heart, primarily he was a farmer. His farm was located about two miles from the coke works. Much to his annoyance, however, Hill and his farmhands regularly were encountering large objects "worthy of some antiquarian." A local commentator, George H. Thurston, remarked that for years when walking over the property, Hill usually found objects resembling "gigantic human bones." Hill had concluded that he possessed a veritable "cemetery of giants."

The greater majority of such "bones" were unearthed while plowing the fields. Despite his efforts not to publicize such discoveries reports soon were circulating locally. Unfortunately for him, though, the farm stood directly upon a busy public road. Accordingly, numerous souvenir hunters kept turning up, much to Hill's disgust. By 1855, Hill assembled a work crew to gather systematically all of those "curious items." During this project, he also undertook an informal inventory of what was being assembled.

He reported that one apparent thigh bone was a foot longer than any belonging to a modern adult human. And many of the jawbones were of such size that "passed with ease over the largest . . . head and face and extended [even] behind the back of the head." In any case, a large wagon later hauled everything to an old apple orchard at the back of his property. These bones were stacked there for about three years. Nonetheless, intruders eventually found their way to the orchard. Consequently, he eventually arranged that the "bone horde" be buried within a large pit. That ended the trespassing problem.

Meanwhile, while clearing away some brush, Hill's workmen made another puzzling discovery. They had found what appeared to be a large iron collar. As Thurston remarked, "This ring had attached . . . at six points, as many short rudely wrought and heavy iron chains, each having . . . a large iron collar with a section . . . working on a hinge . . . as to admit an opening on each collar." He added that this contraption had been discovered "under some large rocks and was much rusted." No one had the slightest idea about either the origins or purpose of this object. Hill speculated that this finding related to some ancient, unknown Native American tribe.

All those bones probably were the remains of prehistoric mammals, such as mammoths and giant ground sloths, which had populated North America amid the last Ice Age. But Hill and his associates had concluded that such remains were of human origins. In 1858, the scientific discipline of paleontology was in its preliminary stage. For instance, scientists had become aware of dinosaurs only a decade earlier. Both Hill and Thurston ascribed to the conventional wisdom of that period. A more sophisticated awareness would not be prevalent for another fifty years. Various observers began speculating about what other "unknown wonders" would be found within the Youghiogheny Valley.

Thurston believed that similar finds would not be possible for much longer. He declared that the "obliterating tracks of business" already were "filling up every foot of this beautiful valley." Nonetheless, this writer is curious whether any memories of these discoveries on Hill's farm remain within local folklore. Those interred bones probably have remained underground to this day. Does anyone know the origins of that large iron object? Anyway, whatever became of it?

A Vital Rail Link

DURING THE first decades of the 19th Century, coal mining became the main industry within the vicinity of the Youghiogheny River. Throughout the Ohio Valley, commercial buyers considered "Youghiogheny Coal" to be a high-quality commodity. Initially, most of this coal was transported down the river by barge. The advent of the railroads [circa 1850] obviously introduced a faster freight delivery method. Accordingly, a group of entrepreneurs organized the Pittsburgh and Connellsville Railroad, the first rail line to run along the Youghiogheny.

By all accounts, the chief investors mainly were influential western Pennsylvania businessmen. The major exception, though, was William Henry Aspinwall, a steamship magnate from New York City. He was intent upon establishing a system of "internal improvements" within the United States. A major local figure was James B. Corey, an early western Pennsylvania "coal baron," who owned real property, containing coal deposits, near Connellsville. He was also an original partner in the Westmoreland Coal Company. The railroad company's initial president was William Larimer, Jr., who was well-versed in matters relating to overland transportation. He had owned a Conestoga wagon company carrying freight between Philadelphia and Pittsburgh.

Although he had been following the progress of canal construction around Pennsylvania, Larimer sensed railroads would be the paramount mode for commercial shipping. Larimer's interest in this railroad was due to being another major Westmoreland Coal shareholder. During the Civil War [1861-1865] Larimer attained the rank of brigadier general within the Federal Army.

A major motivation for establishing the Pittsburgh and Connellsville Railroad was the activities of another railway. During the 1830s the Baltimore and Ohio [B&O] Railroad successfully had been constructing a track route through the Allegheny Mountains. The aim had been to connect the Chesapeake Bay region with the Ohio River Valley. Furthermore, the investors, mostly from Baltimore, were intent upon creating a rail link with the growing cities around the Great Lakes. By 1834, the B&O had reached Harper's Ferry, Virginia. Eight years later the track line had been completed to Cumberland, Maryland. Most observers concluded that the line would be reaching Connellsville within a few years.

Meanwhile, construction work was beginning for the Pittsburgh and Connellsville, with the intention from the beginning of being a two-track line. The tracks were to run from downtown Pittsburgh along the Monongahela River's eastern bank toward McKeesport. At that point, the trains were to follow generally the Youghiogheny's eastern shore all the way to Connellsville, an approximate distance of forty-five miles. The builders were careful to utilize a 4'8 ½ track gauge, favored by the Baltimore and Ohio. In railroad parlance, the gauge comprises the distance between the inside rail edges and the locomotive's corresponding wheel span. During the antebellum period, various American railways often used different gauges, thereby causing problems when moving freight from one road to another.

Although the line had reached McKeesport by 1850, a series of financial setbacks began hindering operations. For instance, Aspinwall had severed all connections with the company, preferring to concentrate on other business interests. They had problems, moreover, securing financial loans from local bankers. This problem was alleviated somewhat when Judge Thomas Mellon showed interest. Mellon was agreeable, in 1855, that Henry Blackstone of Connellsville would become the company's general superintendent.

Despite the intervention of T. Mellon and Sons Bank, a major national economic downturn in 1857, created a dire fiscal emergency. The "Panic of 1857" almost forced the company into bankruptcy and logistical problems periodically disrupted construction. Several weeks after the start of the Civil War, in April 1861, the railroad finally reached Connellsville. Throughout the war years, therefore, the Pittsburgh and Connellsville transported freight, especially coal along the route.

The coal was being shipped to the Pittsburgh iron mills and foundries engaged in war production. Along the rail line was a series of coal mines which provided fuel to the passing trains. And the company owned several of those mines that stood nearby to the local stations. Furthermore, the railway began passenger service during this period, causing fewer persons to ride upon the steam packets traversing the Youghiogheny.

By 1871, the Baltimore and Ohio Railroad had reached Connellsville. The corporate president, John W. Garrett, was aboard the first train to arrive in town. Garrett quickly arranged for the building of a spur line running between Connellsville to Morgantown, West Virginia. Popular opinion held that a merger between the lines was inevitable. But that development did not occur for several more years.

Meanwhile, Henry Clay Frick had opened his coke works, consisting of fifty beehive ovens, upon 123 acres of land at

Broadford. He had built those "blazing igloos" through several generous loans from T. Mellon and Sons Bank. Subsequently, Judge Mellon approved additional monies permitting Frick to construct a local spur line connecting his property with the Pittsburgh and Connellsville.

Mellon, and Frick, were instrumental in assisting Garrett in his efforts to conclude a merger between the two railroads. Although the Pittsburgh and Connellsville retained its corporate name until 1875, the track route became a vital link within the Baltimore and Ohio Railroad network. Accordingly, by 1880, those Connellsville residents boarding a passenger train at the local station had the potential of ending their sojourns in distant cities, including Chicago and St. Louis.

Saints Along the Youghiogheny

MOST READERS are familiar with the Church of Jesus Christ of the Latter-Day Saints, popularly known as the Mormons. Furthermore, the headquarters of this branch of Christianity has been in Salt Lake City, Utah since 1846. Over the years, though, several schisms have occurred within their ranks. One such group in western Pennsylvania, in 1858, organized the Church of Jesus Christ in West Elizabeth, a town across the Monongahela River from Elizabeth. Like their Utah counterparts, they preferred to be known as the "Saints." By 1858, they had decided to establish themselves upon the Youghiogheny, nearby the village of Greenock within Elizabeth Township.

While the Latter-Day Saints were in Nauvoo, Illinois in the early 1840s, the church founder, Joseph Smith, Sr., claimed that a divine revelation had sanctioned the practice of polygamy. His advocacy of men having several wives got him into grave legal trouble with the Illinois state authorities. By June 1844, Smith and several senior church leaders were in jail at Carthage, Illinois. On June 27, an angry mob attacked the jail and murdered Smith.

Not surprisingly, Smith's death caused a leadership crisis within the movement. Brigham Young, the senior member of the Council of Apostles, claimed to be his logical successor. A strong proponent of polygamy, Young eventually led most of the membership out to the Great Salt Lake in Utah. A sizeable minority, though, recognized the hereditary leadership of Joseph Smith, Jr., and opposed polygamy. Settling in Independence, Missouri, they became known as the Reorganized Church of Jesus Christ of Latter Day Saints. But one major church leader, Sydney Rigdon, wanted no part of either group.

An outspoken foe of polygamy, Rigdon also detested Young. Accordingly, Rigdon and a core following formed their own denomination, based upon Smith's original tenants. After relocating to northern Pennsylvania, they made their headquarters at Greencastle in Franklin County. Unfortunately, though, Rigdon, a former Baptist minister, lacked the personal qualities to lead a religious movement. Wishing a quiet life, about 1850, Rigdon and his family moved to Kentucky. His death on October 20, 1876, at Friendship, New York largely went unnoticed.

As Rigdon's influence waned, his followers looked for someone to fill the void. One group recognized the spiritual leadership of William Bickerton, a former Methodist lay preacher from Monongahela City, Pennsylvania. By May 1861, he had become the president of the Church of Jesus Christ with headquarters in West Elizabeth. Although they attempted reconciliation with the main church in Salt Lake City, they could not abide polygamy. Consequently, Bickerton soon broke all dialogue with the "Utah Church.". Within a public document, President Bickerton announced that his group was severing all connections with the Latter-Day Saints "because of their adultery and general wickedness." They always, therefore, indignantly repudiated the sobriquet of *Mormon*. But Bickerton and the others continued to accept most of Joseph Smith's basic teachings.

They subsequently established various "Branches" in communities around western Pennsylvania. As with the Utah Church, the members preferred to address each other as either "brother" or "sister." And they annually convened a General Conference at one of the branches. In January 1858, at the General Conference held in Pine Run [now Clairton], they voted to establish a new church at Greenock, a village along the Youghiogheny River within Elizabeth Township. A meetinghouse was built nearby to the river upon a lot they had bought. The Saints would be operating within a community of farmers, tradesmen, and coal miners.

On December 1860, they assigned William Cadman, Sr. to "labor" in Greenock and establish a viable branch. The following May a General Conference was held within a frame house in Greenock, not far from the river bank. On May 6, after the Sabbath "praise service" several new converts, clad in white robes were baptized by immersion within the Youghiogheny, Over the next several years residents, therefore, could witness regularly baptism processionals walking toward the river,

During the first week of July 1862, the General Conference was convened within the unfinished meetinghouse. At this conclave, President Bickerton complained about the unfinished state of the building. Accordingly, Elder Benjamin Meadowcroft made sure that unspecified construction costs were paid to contractors, thereupon assuring the meetinghouse's completion. On July 8, 1863, the Greenock Branch formally consecrated their new sanctuary.

The Church of Jesus Christ also believed in faith healing through the laying on of hands by senior elders. Consequently, they often included this ritual within their worship services. For instance, on January 17, 1864, Martha James Lyons from upriver in West Newton purportedly regained her speech. She apparently had lacked oral abilities for almost a year. Several months later Lyons was baptized into the Church of Jesus Christ.

During the spring of 1870, a memorable incident occurred late one Sunday afternoon. Between services five Greenock

Branch members had crossed the Youghiogheny within a flat-bottomed rowboat to have dinner at a friend's house. About 5:00 P.M., they were rowing back over to attend the customary evening service. They were the following: William and Elizabeth Cadman; James and Sarah Russell; and James Louitt. Upon reaching mid-stream, however, a sudden fierce thunderstorm ensued. Strong winds, and high waves, threatened to capsize them into the river. James Russell later recalled that they appeared about to drown rather than "lay safely on the shore." Amid their frightening ordeal, they began singing old hymns. Meanwhile, Elder George Barnes was watching the impending tragedy over in Greenock. The desperate Barnes "rebuked the wind in the name of the Lord Jesus Christ." As he was uttering this prayer the storm conveniently moved on. Consequently, the rowboat occupants reached their destination without further trouble.

The following year the annual General Conference was held at Greenock during the first week of July. The participants apparently were delighted with the progress made in the Youghiogheny Valley over the last few years. Within a week, however, a major fire destroyed the meetinghouse. Recently returned from a trip to Zanesville, Ohio, President Bickerton summoned an emergency conference in West Elizabeth. Although the charred ruins already had been dismantled, they decided not to rebuild the sanctuary. Upon Bickerton's recommendation, moreover, they voted to relocate across the river to the town of Coulterville [Coulter] where several members resided. A down payment on a vacant lot there was made three weeks later. But they also continued to retain their Greenock real property.

For the next two years, the Coulterville members met within a vacant warehouse. They repeatedly assured Bickerton that "every honorable and lawful effort" was being made to raise the funds for the meetinghouse. For some reason, though, they were incapable of achieving this goal. In July 1874, the remnants of the Greenock Branch hosted a General Conference at Mount Vernon School House, located in Elizabeth Township several miles from the old meetinghouse. At this session, the decision was made to sell their Greenock property. And they decided to abandon the effort of establishing a Coulterville Branch. This action effectively ended the Church of Jesus Christ upon the Youghiogheny.

Instead, they had decided to concentrate their western Pennsylvania activities within the Monongahela Valley. At a General Conference at West Elizabeth, in April 1878, Elder William Skillen reported that all the Youghiogheny properties finally had been sold. Since that time the Church of Jesus Christ has maintained a constant presence at Monongahela City which persists to this day.

A Noted Local Figure

DURING ITS two centuries of history, the borough of Elizabeth has been associated with figures who distinguished themselves in both state and national affairs. One of these personages was General James A. Ekin, who is mostly unknown to current Elizabeth residents. Although James Adams Ekin, Jr. was born in Pittsburgh, on August 13, 1819, he belonged to a family with deep connections to Elizabeth. His mother, Susan Bayard, was the daughter of the town's founders, Colonel Stephen and Elizabeth Mackay Bayard, Susan had left her birthplace in 1814, however, when she married James Adams Ekin, Sr., of Pittsburgh. Despite never knowing personally his maternal grandparents, Ekin's lifelong goal was to uphold their legacy of success. A desire to be near his ancestral roots prompted Ekin to move permanently to Elizabeth in 1840.

From his youth, Ekin was interested in both military affairs and history. For nearly two decades "Colonel" Ekin was the commanding officer of the "Forks' Soldiery," a local militia battalion based within the Monongahela River Valley. Accordingly, through this position, Ekin actively participated within the festivities, in 1848, which honored Senator Henry Clay of Kentucky while he was traveling by steamboat along the

Monongahela from Brownsville to Pittsburgh. As Clay's vessel traveled passed Elizabeth, Ekin commanded the artillery battery that repeatedly fired cannon salutes to this venerable American statesman.

Meanwhile, Ekin followed the family tradition by pursuing a career within the local boat building industry. He assumed a management position with Walker and Stephens Company, the leading boat construction firm in Elizabeth. During the "peak years" [1830- 1860] there were three boat works in Elizabeth along the Monongahela riverfront. Any river traveler, in 1850, often would have seen six steamboat hulls mounted upon large blocks in various building phases. During the years prior to the Civil War, many of those boats were traveling regularly along the Mississippi River and its tributaries.

When Ekin joined the company his uncle, Samuel Walker, primarily ran the business. By 1857, though, the Walker family had decided to divest themselves of much of their controlling stock. And it was Ekin who bought them out. During the years he ran the company, thirty large steam riverboats were constructed. And several of those vessels reportedly were among the finest ever built at the local yards. Ekins's active supervision over the company a major stockholder within that enterprise concluded, in June 1861, when he entered active military duty. For many years, however, Ekin remained a major stockholder in that enterprise, and continued to own real properties around Elizabeth.

During his early adulthood, Ekin had been a firm partisan of the Democratic Party. But he became disenchanted with them because the Democrats temporized on the slavery issue. Accordingly, in 1858, he participated within a meeting in Pittsburgh which created formally the Republican Party in western Pennsylvania. Two years later he supported Abraham Lincoln's successful presidential candidacy. With the outbreak of the Civil War, in April 1861, Ekin volunteered to serve within the Federal Army. By April 23, he reported for duty with the 12th Pennsylvania Infantry.

Although he wanted combat duty, Colonel Ekin was installed as chief regimental quartermaster. Despite frequent attempts to secure a field infantry command, he remained a quartermaster throughout the Civil War. While his main tour of duty was in Indianapolis, Indiana, he did spend some months supervising the Allegheny Arsenal in Pittsburgh. Ekin's superiors, notably Major General Daniel F. Sickles, commended him for his capable service, and his honest handling of large military procurement funds. By November 1863, the War Department transferred him to Washington, D.C. where he assumed various top posts within the Office of Quartermaster General. Because of his good record, Ekin became a trusted advisor to both President Lincoln and Secretary of War Edwin Stanton. Through these close connections, therefore, Ekin was involved heavily in the events following Lincoln's assassination, on April 14, 1865.

Ekin was selected by President Andrew Johnson, to serve within the honor guard conveying Lincoln's remains back to Springfield, Illinois for final internment. Upon his return to the District of Columbia, he was appointed to the military tribunal which tried John Wilkes Booth's surviving accomplices. Believing the evidence was circumstantial, Ekin argued that clemency be granted to Mary Surratt, the sole woman implicated in the Lincoln assassination. To his disappointment, though, he was overruled and she was among four defendants hanged. Recent scholarship, though, has confirmed that Mrs. Surrat was well-aware of Booth's plot. In fact, throughout the war, her boardinghouse had been a "safe house" for Confederate secret agents operating in the national capital

Unlike many of his fellow officers, Colonel Ekin chose to remain on active duty after the war. By executive order, in April 1870, President Ulysses S. Grant promoted him to the rank of Brevet Brigadier General. That rank was made permanent two years later. By 1876, he had been elevated to serve as Deputy Quartermaster General of the Army. And he received the additional assignment of Chief Quartermaster, Federal Department of the South, which required several years of residence in San Antonio, Texas, supervising a large military supply depot.

During a belated visit to Elizabeth in May 1871, General Ekin's old neighbors prepared a lavish welcome. The steamboat transporting him also brought a large group of civic leaders from Pittsburgh. At the head of a parade was the carriage carrying Ekin and his close local relatives. After a formal welcoming ceremony, Ekin was feted with a testimonial banquet. Except for a few brief trips in later years, this junket was Ekin's last direct contact with his old hometown

After twenty-two years of active service, in 1883, General Ekin finally retired. Subsequently, he moved to Louisville, Kentucky to reside with his daughter, Mrs. Mary Elizabeth Willson and her family. His son-in-law. August E. Willson was an active politician, once serving a term as Kentucky's governor. On March 27, 1891, Ekin [77 yrs.] died in Louisville following a brief illness His funeral was held at the First Presbyterian Church of Louisville, where he had served as an Elder for some years. Despite his longtime wish to be interred in Elizabeth, his family decided to forgo this option, Instead, he was buried within Cave Hill Cemetery in Louisville.

News of Ekin's passing was met with great sadness in Elizabeth and other nearby communities. His death permanently severed a vital link with the town's founders, Stephen and Elizabeth Bayard. Residents marked his death by holding a series of memorial services in the various local churches. Several years later the borough council honored this native son by naming one of its arteries, Ekin Street. In 2019, this Elizabeth roadway continues to bear this surname making it the only tangible memorial to Brigadier General James Adams Ekin that has survived.

Bulldozing Upon the River

AMID THE last several winters residents have noticed that various sections of the local rivers sometimes are frozen with ice. Although not too common these days, this was a regular occurrence in the 19th Century. This icing was a serious threat, moreover, to any boat attempting to traverse either the Youghiogheny or Monongahela Rivers during the winter months. The various local mining enterprises did not cease operating when the weather was bad. Knowing that "Youghiogheny Coal" was prized throughout the Ohio River Valley, the mine operators continued to convey that precious commodity by barge.

That activity, though, usually was forestalled when thick ice blocked the channels. They became interested, therefore, upon hearing a rumor that a resident of Elizabeth, Pennsylvania, in 1876, had invented an ice-breaking device known as a "bulldozer." By all accounts, 19th Century winters were consistently colder than today. Consequently, all the western Pennsylvania waterways gained solid ice covers throughout the winter. This was especially true in the decades before various pollutants, notably Sulphur and iron oxide, began accumulating upon the channel bottoms. Those substances were by-products of the many mining operations operating along the Youghiogheny, and other local rivers. Accordingly, neither the barges nor the towboats could venture any distance.

Sojourners traveling along the rivers, therefore, would have noticed large numbers of vessels docked at any boat landing. Those boats were protected by "ice breakers" which consisted of abutments placed within the waters near the shore above the docks. Such structures were large log cribs filled with rocks, and other debris. These breakers were meant to preclude big chunks of floating ice and logs from colliding with the stationary boats.

With the advent of warmer weather, the ice began to break up and heavy rainfall commenced. Consequently, the water levels of the rivers began rising to serious levels. And the swollen waters carried large ice blocks around those breakers, thereby causing the boats to be stranded within their "snug harbors." Under such circumstances, the usual solution was to create some opening adjacent to the stranded vessels. But this was a dubious proposition when the ice became too thick. As the historian Richard T. Wiley once observed: "And it was not always effective . . . because the thickness often left no room for the lateral movement of the floating ice." In February 1877, unusually large ice flows caused great damage along both the Youghiogheny and Monongahela Rivers. A considerable number of steamboats, towboats, and barges were struck by some "mini-icebergs."

An Elizabeth coal operator, John Nixon O'Neill, lost a towboat and three barges that winter at his Monongahela wharf near town. Unwilling to sustain similar losses during the following winter, he took positive action. O'Neill created a new device capable of crushing thick ice. He constructed a heavy timber object thirty feet in length on each side, and six feet in depth. Except for the front it was vertical on all sides. This structure also was sloped backward from the top to the portion below water. The inventor bent down heavy iron rails which he attached firmly in front. With this object, he deposited a heavy stone load that upon release could drop deeply into the river.

With the first river ice, in January 1878, O'Neill lashed his invention to a large towboat. A big crowd of onlookers in Elizabeth watched as the vessel moved steadily through the ice. The attached device crushed all the ice that was encountered. Large pieces of flowing ice were demolished into smaller chunks which flowed on harmlessly. Accordingly, open channels were created along both banks for some distance. Over the next three months, O'Neill repeatedly duplicated his initial demonstration at other locales along the Monongahela. By April 12, local newspapers happily declared that only a few vessels within the Monongahela River Valley had been lost that winter.

During the late 19th Century the term "bulldozing" was common within American political slang. This sobriquet usually was applied to ruthless politicians who defeated their opponents into submission. Consequently, O'Neill utilized the name "bulldozer" for his invention. Most western Pennsylvanians apparently agreed with him.

Within a few years, other local entrepreneurs had their own bulldozers. Throughout the Monongahela Valley, coal mining operators were using bulldozers when serious river ice developed. They were able, therefore, to keep their barges from being damaged and they could get their coal cargoes downriver in winter. Bulldozers came into common use upon the Youghiogheny River. By 1890, bulldozing devices could be found all along the Ohio River system. John Nixon O'Neill did not make money from his invention because he failed to apply for a federal patent. And he did not gain lasting fame either for his efforts.

The Distinguished Senator Cowan

THROUGHOUT EARLY 1861 West Newton residents were worried about the future of the United States. With Abraham Lincoln's election to the presidency, in November 1860, various southern states had seceded from the Federal Union. There was some good news, though, during this uncertain period. The Pennsylvania General Assembly had elected Edgar Cowan, a Westmoreland County resident, to fill a vacant U.S. Senate seat. And everyone knew that he was married to Lucretia Oliver, a West Newton native.

Edgar Cowan was born, on September 9, 1815, in Greensburg, Pennsylvania. Upon graduating from Franklin College in 1839, he began reading law under the direction of Walter S. Forward, a leading Pittsburgh attorney. Two years later he married Lucretia Oliver, the daughter of James B. Oliver, among West Newton's most prominent citizens. After admission to the Westmoreland County Bar in 1842, he commenced successful law practice in Greensburg.

An admirer of Senator Henry Clay of Kentucky, Cowan was a supporter of the Whig Party. He attended the national Whig convention, in December 1839, at Harrisburg, Pennsylvania. While preferring Clay's candidacy, Cowan later supported the eventual Whig nominee, William Henry Harrison of Indiana, who won the presidential election of 1840. For the next fifteen years, he remained active in state party affairs. In June 1852, during a Whig party event in Pittsburgh, he initially met Abraham Lincoln, a former Illinois congressman.

During those years, moreover, Cowan enjoyed a notable legal career. He was regarded as among the best courtroom lawyers west of the Allegheny Mountains. Cowan liked to observe that usually, it was "the best story told in court" which won the case. In any case, he was on legal retainer with the Pittsburgh and Connellsville Railroad. By 1856, the Whig Party nationally had become politically divided over the slavery issue. Although no abolitionist, Cowan was not pro-slavery. Accordingly, he switched his loyalties to the new Republican Party, and backed Lincoln's successful 1860 campaign. In September 1860, with the sudden retirement of U.S. Senator William Bigler, state Republicans began looking for a potential successor, someone known to be moderate on the slavery question. The senior Pennsylvania senator, Simon Cameron, suggested that Cowan would be a good choice. Prior to the ratification of the 17th Amendment [April 3, 1913], the respective state legislatures elected all federal senators. Consequently, in February 1861, Cowan easily defeated a Democratic challenger, Henry Foster.

Senator Cowan officially took office, on March 4, 1861, approximately one month before the commencement of the Civil War. When Cameron was appointed secretary of war by President Lincoln, his Senate seat became vacant. Cowan was not pleased, though, when David Wilmont, an old political enemy, became Cameron's successor. Not surprisingly, the two new colleagues never managed to establish a good working relationship. Throughout his senatorial years, moreover, Cowan was regarded as a "political maverick" by the Republican leadership.

He faithfully supported all legislation that militarily furthered the war effort. Cowan believed the primary war aim was preserving the Federal Union. He did not believe, however, that Congress possessed the constitutional authority to abolish slavery. Instead, he argued that the respective state governments held that power. He consistently opposed legislative measures dealing with slavery emancipation. Otherwise, on most economic issues Cowan loyally voted with his party.

Nonetheless, in the spring of 1863, Cowan broke with his party on a major controversy. On March 10, Senator Marvin S. Wilkinson of Minnesota introduced a motion calling for the expulsion of a senior Democratic senator, Jesse D. Bright of Indiana. That lawmaker was accused of engaging in seditious dealings with Confederate leaders, including President Jefferson Davis. Believing that much of the evidence was circumstantial, Cowan was among three Republicans who joined with the Democrats in opposition. But the motion passed by a wide margin. No sitting senator has faced a comparable punishment since Bright's ouster.

By April 1863, Republican senatorial colleagues publicly were denouncing Cowan as a "Copperhead," a northerner with southern sympathies. Upon the Senate floor, Benjamin Wade of Ohio described him as a "shameless watchdog of slavery." Although Cowan indignantly repudiated all such assertions, his political position in Pennsylvania steadily deteriorated. During the annual Allegheny County Republican Convention in Pittsburgh, in June 1863, the delegates passed a censure resolution against him. At the urging of Governor Andrew Curtin, moreover, the Lincoln administration excluded Cowan from any major input over federal patronage within Pennsylvania.

Following Lincoln's assassination, on April 14, 1865, Cowan pledged his support to the new president, Andrew Johnson. Unfortunately, though, most of his senatorial colleagues already had disowned him politically. Accordingly, in the congressional election of 1866, he sought reelection as a Democrat. But the

Pennsylvania General Assembly voted to return Simon Cameron to his old Senate seat. In 1867, Secretary of State William Seward proposed that Cowan be appointed U.S. Minister to the Austro-Hungarian Empire. But his vengeful former colleagues, led by Senator Orville Browning of Ohio, blocked the nomination.

After returning to private life, Cowan resumed practicing law in Greensburg, including another stint as legal counsel with the Pittsburgh and Connellsville Railroad. He was helpful, therefore, in completing a merger with the Baltimore and Ohio Railroad in 1875. During his final years failing health forced him into retirement. Upon his death, on August 31, 1885, in Greensburg, Cowan was interred within St. Clair Cemetery. Several years later the former senator was recognized posthumously when the village of Cowansburg in Sewickley Township was named in his honor.

The Battle of Buena Vista

ATRADITION WITHIN Allegheny County has been that during the 19th Century, the village of Buena Vista in Elizabeth Township experienced a bloody shootout. The primary combatants were striking coal miners arrayed against a group of imported strikebreakers. Beyond those basic facts, though, little else about the "Battle of Buena Vista" is remembered. This notable fight which occurred along the Youghiogheny River, on November 29, 1874, purportedly resulting in several deaths. This battle climaxed a series of ugly incidents that began when miners initiated a strike against the Armstrong Coal Works.

Normally, most of those workers crossed the Youghiogheny daily into Westmoreland County to labor in Charles S. Armstrong's mine. Although he consistently refused to bargain, since August 1874, they had been demanding that Armstrong grant them a wage increase of four cents per hour. Accordingly, the miners initiated a strike before Armstrong implemented a threatened lockout. Many observers believed the miners were commencing their walkout at a bad time. At that point, the United States was experiencing a severe economic downturn known as the "Long Depression." This business crisis had begun in September 1873, with the collapse of a major Philadelphia bank, Jay Cooke and Company. The ensuing depression disrupted the national economy for seven years.

Despite the depression, the Miners' National Association [MNA], led by President John Siney, began a concerted organizing effort within the western Pennsylvania coalfields. They placed a strong priority upon recruiting miners working for the numerous coal operations along the Youghiogheny. The *National Labor Tribune*, edited in Pittsburgh by Thomas A. Armstrong, ran several articles about s successful recruiting campaign at the Osceola Coal Works, a major enterprise across the Youghiogheny from the village of Greenock in Elizabeth Township.

The MNA's organizers initially paid scant attention to the Armstrong Works until they heard reports that the miners working there wanted to organize. Although Armstrong's company was not large, it did employ much of the available local workforce. Moreover, Armstrong was a coal supplier for the Pittsburgh and Connellsville Railroad which ran directly in front of the mine. A large coal bin stood adjacent to the local stop, Armstrong Station. Accordingly, once the strike began, on September 10, the Pittsburgh and Connellsville aided Armstrong by transporting without charge a party of scabs [strikebreakers] from Pittsburgh out to his mine.

After the walkout had begun, Armstrong dispatched an agent to New York City to recruit "replacement" workers from the New York Italian Labor Company. Most of them were unemployed recent Italian immigrants, barely conversant in English. Under their supervisor, Fredrick Guscetti, on October 5, the main party reached the mine. They were quartered within a cluster of cabins adjoining the mine, with armed sentries posted to protect them from any surprise attacks. When they began work the following morning, they were subjected to loud verbal denunciations from the strikers watching from across the river. Not surprisingly, the strikers enjoyed strong support from the residents of the various other Youghiogheny towns. The citizenry socially ostracized all of Armstrong's scabs and local merchants refused to conduct business with them. The hostile attitudes manifested by both sides eventually led to violence.

About 9:00 P.M., on October 29, several scabs defiantly entered James Lloyd's grocery in Buena Vista. A few minutes later they were expelled from Lloyd's place following a scuffle with strike sympathizers. Apparently, no further major incidents occurred for the next month. But on Saturday, November 28, about 7:00 P.M., five strikebreakers entered Buena Vista looking for a fight. In any case, they soon encountered several angry strikers in front of Gault's Drug Store. Amid the ensuing brawl, one scab, Charles Moses, was stabbed in the groin, while a companion, Frank Mora, received an ugly scalp wound. Upon learning of this episode, Guscetti and his men seized firearms from Armstrong's storeroom. For the next twelve hours, they fired sporadic volleys at random visible targets around Buena Vista. As a precaution, the strikers posted armed sentries to spread the alarm if anyone crossed the river.

Around 9:00 A.M., Guscetti and several others appeared in town evidently seeking a local physician, Dr. R.S. Stewart, to treat their wounded comrades. As they approached Stewart's house, some vigilantes ambushed them near the schoolhouse. Under intense gunfire, they promptly retreated to a large barge. Subsequently, more armed villagers reinforced the original pursuers. At that point, unfounded rumors circulated that Guscetti's men were planning to burn down all of Buena Vista.

The leading town citizen, William A. Bell, later justified his neighbors' violence, telling a reporter from the *National Labor Tribune*, "The villagers acted entirely on the defensive and would not have fired had they not been satisfied that the intruders meant harm." Once the shooting commenced Buena Vista's women and children were sent to safe locations. Some took refuge in Frank Patterson's large frame house, whereas others congregated within the spacious Bell Mansion. Meanwhile, most male residents gathered at the gristmill where they selected Frank Patterson and Stewart Osborne as their "captains."

While couriers on horseback rode out in search of reinforcements, and ammunition, other villagers pursued the scabs back to their barge. Several snipers had taken positions on the opposite bank to protect Guscetti's retreat. Their shots seriously wounded at least two of the pursuers. By the time Patterson and the main contingent had reached the riverbank, the barge was mid-stream. Nearly forty guns were fired at the barge occupants, with deadly results. Three of Guscetti's men were killed instantly. The remainder of the men, several of them wounded, quickly dove into the river. Upon reaching the opposite shore, however, they found that the situation remained dangerous because the gunfire from Buena Vista remained intense.

Although several of them, including Guscetti, eventually reached the high ground, the others found cover within a large drainage ditch by the railroad tracks. Nobody apparently noted that the barge, carrying three corpses, was drifting aimlessly downstream. By noon, over 500 heavily armed men were in Buena Vista. Contingents from most of the neighboring Youghiogheny communities had reached the scene, while local farmers showed their support by supplying food provisions. William A. Bell, a prominent merchant, dispatched a couple of transport wagons to McKeesport to procure additional ammunition. At this point, Patterson deployed this imposing fighting force along the river.

Meanwhile, on the opposite side of the river, their desperate opponents had built barricades around their cabins to make a final stand. Most of the 150 scabs had assumed positions behind any object that afforded protection from the bullets. On the Buena Vista side, though, the combatants did not contemplate a direct assault. Accordingly, for several hours an uneasy stand-off existed, regularly highlighted by sniper fire. Most casualties occurred during this interlude.

About 4:00 P.M., approximately fifty horsemen, led by Humphrey Campbell, forded the Youghiogheny about a mile downstream. Several observers later recalled that one of them was brandishing an American flag as he rode. They ultimately assumed positions upon the hillside behind the scabs' cabins. With their adversaries now in a potentially deadly crossfire, they demanded Guscetti's surrender. Consequently, his wife emerged from a cabin waving a white flag fastened to a rifle barrel. Following a protracted debate, the dejected scabs gave up their weaponry. They were marched off at gunpoint toward Armstrong's largest warehouse. They were to depart when the first available northern bound train passed through Armstrong Station on Monday.

Since late morning Armstrong, and local officials had been sending telegrams to law enforcement authorities in Pittsburgh. Sheriff Walter Hare of Allegheny County and a dozen special deputies arrived in Buena Vista several hours after the fighting had ceased. He was shocked to find that five men were dead, along with thirty wounded. A serious amount of property damage had occurred, notably, buildings riddled with bullet holes. A myriad of spent cartridges littered the entire area.

For the record, the drifting barge finally was intercepted three miles downriver at the village of Stringtown in Elizabeth Township. The three bodies eventually were loaded into a transport wagon, bound for McKeesport. The deceased ultimately were interred within Saint Joseph's Catholic Cemetery in McKeesport.

Sheriff Hare assigned Chief Deputy Hugh M. Fife as a liaison with Westmoreland County officials to assure the scabs' orderly evacuation aboard a Pittsburgh and Connellsville freight train the next morning. Word out of Pittsburgh soon reached Buena Vista that many of them now were working at a mine in Trumball County, Ohio. As the *Pittsburgh Post* commented: "It is hoped that wherever they may go, we shall have no more of the bloody scenes that were witnessed in Buena Vista." To his enemies' amusement Armstrong became embroiled in a noisy public quarrel with Guscetti. Apparently, the mine owner had failed to pay those scabs about $700 in back wages.

Despite the convening of an Allegheny County Grand Jury, on January 20, 1875, no participants ever were convicted for their roles in the "Battle of Buena Vista." By February 1875, Armstrong had agreed that the wage dispute be placed before an arbitrator for final settlement. The umpire finally ruled that the strikers were entitled to a two cents per hour pay raise. Following this ruling, the miners promptly returned to work.

This bloody episode soon was forgotten by most outsiders. The Armstrong Works operated until 1900 when a major fire forced its permanent closing. Residents later claimed that the blaze continued throughout much of the 20th Century. Moreover, they said that on rainy days steam still could be seen coming out of various hillside galleries [openings] of the old mine. Although local memories of the "Battle of Buena Vista" have faded, a few elderly Elizabeth Township residents readily recalled that event, as late as 1985, to this writer in several oral history interviews.

A Youghiogheny River Tragedy

THROUGHOUT THE latter weeks of May 1890, the residents of the Youghiogheny River Valley were enduring a prolonged heat wave. About 9:00 A.M., on May 24, an African American teenager, Cora Jackson, [15 yrs.], who resided nearby to Collinsburg, was intending to take a trip. She planned to visit her older brother, Caleb Jackson, who lived downriver at Alpsville. Unfortunately, though, she never returned from this sojourn.

Unable to afford a rail ticket from the Pittsburgh and Lake Erie [P&LE] Railroad which had a station in Collinsburg, Cora was traveling by rowboat, a common option in that era. Throughout the 19th Century, numerous people could be seen rowing upon the Youghiogheny. And they shared the river with steam towboats pushing coal barges from the local mines. Any vessel heading northward had the advantage of going with the current toward the Youghiogheny's mouth at McKeesport. Miss Jackson probably had made this trip on many occasions. The distance between Collinsburg and Alpsville was about eight miles, Jackson reached her destination without incident.

She spent most of the next three days visiting with her relatives. Alpsville was a coal mining hamlet next to the larger town of Coulterville [Coulter]. Around noon, on May 27, she began her return trip upriver to Collinsburg. Upon traveling southward, however, any boat was going against the current. She probably did not experience much difficulty before approaching a major eddy at Robbins Station. The waters from a sizeable stream, Crawford's Run, were of such volume from a freshet that the rowboat began a pronounced shaking. Apparently, she lost control of her right oar. An eyewitness on shore reported that the boat tipped while she was reaching for the floating oar. Consequently, she pitched forward into the Youghiogheny, surfacing three times before sinking permanently.

Searchers later scoured both banks for any sign of the victim. After several hours, though, they called off the dragnet. Residents surmised that the body had been caught by the current and swept downstream. The situation remained static for the next several days until the body resurfaced nearby to the village of Boston within Elizabeth Township.

During the afternoon of June 1, employees of the Boston Brick Yard noticed an unusual object floating in the river. Moreover, the steamboat *Boston* was within the vicinity. Since November 1876, this fast little steamer had been traveling regularly between McKeesport and Alpsville. Upon reaching that spot, Captain Joseph Waltower ordered his crew to retrieve this object with grappling hooks. A deckhand, Charles Osborne, pulled aboard a decomposed corpse. The general belief around Boston correctly was that the remains belonged to Miss Jackson. Nonetheless, her brother was summoned from Alpsville to render a positive identification.

The next morning the local magistrate, Squire William L. Douglass, convened a special inquest at the Boston schoolhouse. The Allegheny County coroner in Pittsburgh periodically authorized him to hold such hearings. Within thirty minutes Douglass had ruled that Cora Jackson had died, due to accidental drowning. Douglass's main concern was dealing with the serious physical deterioration of the body. She already had been placed within a plain wooden coffin by an undertaker. The current heatwave allowed scant delay in arranging final internment. Transporting her remains by train to Collinsburg was not considered to be desirable. Quite likely, she was interred locally at the Mount Vernon Cemetery.

Although Jackson's drowning was reported within the various western Pennsylvania newspapers, memories of this tragedy were short-lived. But the death did remind locals that the Youghiogheny could be a dangerous waterway. This river hardly was a harmless "big muddy creek." This is a reality which modern Youghiogheny River enthusiasts should recall when seeking recreation upon its waters.

A Crime Spree by Train

AMID THE final decades of the 19th Century, the Youghiogheny River Valley experienced substantial economic growth. This trend is demonstrated by the large number of coal enterprises operating there during these years. Inevitably, the regional population grew and new "coal towns" came into existence. Several of these villages were created by the various coal companies to house their workers. Although most of the newcomers were respectable citizens, a few criminals also showed up.

By 1896, the United States was within the fourth year of severe economic depression. Despite some signs that a recovery was underway, unemployment still was high within the Youghiogheny coalfields. As a means of alleviating their poverty, many idle workers turned to crime. Not surprisingly, it was common knowledge that assorted organized gangs existed in the river towns. Among these criminal rings, the most notorious one was known as the "Russell Gang."

The acknowledged leader of these thugs was an English expatriate. John "Lord Jack" Russell. For nearly three decades this feckless ruffian had committed many crimes throughout western Pennsylvania. Nonetheless, "Lord Jack" usually had managed to evade any official punishment. Possessing a genial demeanor, he was regarded as a minor folk hero among certain segments of the local citizenry. In July 1889, Lord Jack's criminal career ended with his murder in an alley beside a Reynoldton saloon. He was gunned down by an associate during a dispute over sharing the loot gained in a recent robbery. With his passing, the leadership of the gang was assumed by his sons, Samuel and Walter.

Along with the Russell brothers, another gang leader was John "Dude" Parker, a career criminal from McKeesport. He was a participant in the murder of George McClure in Lincoln Township, in 1885, at a locale which came to be known as "Dead Man's Hollow." Although his crony, Walter McConkey, was hanged for this crime, Parker only was charged with manslaughter. He was out of prison within two years of his conviction. Subsequently, Parker was suspected of a series of crimes, especially safe-cracking and armed robbery.

About 7:00 P.M., on August 23, 1896, [Friday] Parker and the Russell brothers robbed James Ward's saloon in McKeesport of seventeen dollars in cash, and several bottles of whiskey. They were observed heading toward the railroad tracks running through the First Ward of McKeesport. Apparently, they climbed aboard a Baltimore and Ohio freight train heading for Connellsville. They disembarked, however, along the tracks within the vicinity of Sutersville, a Westmoreland County river town. Eventually, they crossed the Youghiogheny into Elizabeth Township.

The following afternoon they were loitering near the hamlet of Industry along the Pittsburgh and Lake Erie Railroad [P&LE] tracks when they noticed a stalled train. Sitting on board a gondola [flat] car was a young Finnish immigrant, Nestari Hill, who was returning to McKeesport after visiting friends in Collinsburg. The trio clambered on board and began beating Hill, with the intention of robbing him. After taking his wallet and other valuables, Sam Russell opened the car's trap door.

Several onlookers claimed that they intended to drop their victim onto the tracks below. Fortunately, though, several persons drove the robbers away before that action was complete.

Three hours later the desperadoes were drinking whiskey with several cronies while sitting upon a hill above Scott Haven Station, a P&LE whistle stop. Learning of their presence Squire John McPherson, the local magistrate, sent Constable William A. Miller to arrest them for a recent brawl at Douglass Station. When Miller discovered they were armed with pistols, though, he chose not to confront them. Subsequently, the thugs boasted that they were going to Douglass Station and kill Squire McPherson, a popular local figure. Upon reaching there they found several armed men waiting in ambush. This posse was led by Detective Alvin G. Patterson, a P&LE employee, who had been after them for months.

Upon exchanging gunfire, the fugitives dodged into some nearby woods where they hid for an hour. A disgusted Patterson later complained that a crowd of rail employees, and residents, had watched the skirmish. But they had refused to intervene, thereby allowing the fugitives to escape. Nevertheless, someone reported seeing them climbing onto a freight train traveling toward McKeesport. Patterson then called by telephone various local authorities warning them that some dangerous characters were at large along the Youghiogheny. As the train was passing through Buena Vista, however, they jumped off to board another train that was making a freight stop on a side track.

Meanwhile, Patterson correctly assumed that the fugitives would be switching trains. He requested, therefore, that Constable Stephen Jones stop, and search all rail traffic passing through his village of Boston. A sizeable crowd had been deployed along the tracks as the train carrying the fugitives reached Boston. Upon being discovered, though, the thugs were far from submissive. Although Sam Russell was captured as he ran toward the river, his two companions made their stand by the locomotive. Apparently, Parker shot a young Boston resident, Edward Lewis, in the upper chest. With an enraged crowd in close pursuit, Walter Russell and Parker rushed toward the nearby Boston Bridge.

They entered the bridge tollhouse which caused their pursuers to halt. Along with obtaining sufficient cover, they also took a hostage, Mrs. Grace Hazlet, the toll keeper's wife. The bandits warned the posse that the woman would be shot the moment anyone made an approach. And Constable Jones told his associates that they had found the cartridge boxes that the toll keeper, George Hazlet, kept for protection from would-be robbers. Using Mrs. Hazlet as a human shield, the desperate pair emerged from their shelter. Upon shoving her into a nearby drainage ditch, they made a quick dash for the bridge. Both men successfully crossed the bridge into Versailles Township.

Approximately 200 men joined the manhunt which commenced throughout that locale. The posse members were certain that the fugitives were lurking around one of the many gas derricks to be found within that vicinity. Despite a dragnet lasting all night, the pair apparently had escaped into the heavily wooded hills surrounding Long Run. An informer later claimed that they safely reached a known hideout nearby the village of Guffey.

As the posse was searching the countryside for them, Squire William L. Douglass had to deal with Sam Russell back in Boston. Despite being confined within a storeroom under heavy guard, Douglass did not think the prisoner could be protected from an angry mob. Accordingly, Russell secretly was transferred to McKeesport where he was confined in the Central Police Station. Although professing his innocence, Sam Russell was held on a variety of charges, in lieu of $10,000 bond.

Not surprisingly, rumors spread throughout western Pennsylvania about the exact whereabouts of the two missing desperadoes. They falsely were reported to be in McKeesport, and a dozen other towns. They finally were captured in Munhall, on September 25, by Allegheny County Detective Patrick J. Murphy. Realizing they were surrounded by a heavily armed group, they gave up without a struggle.

After a convalescence, the gondola car victim, Nestari Hill, could resume working at the National Tube Works in McKeesport. Unfortunately, however, Edward Lewis died from his wounds two days following his shooting. Subsequently, in February 1897, John Parker and Walter Russell were hanged for his murder in Pittsburgh. Because he was captured prior to the killing, Samuel Russell was not charged for that crime. But he was sentenced to twenty years imprisonment for the various other criminal acts committed during that violent interlude. Whether he served the entire sentence is not known.

In any case, the elimination of that trio effectively broke the influence of the Russell Gang, because most of their remaining confederates had decided to depart the region. Public tolerance for such lawless activities, moreover, declined after that they went on their spree. While criminal acts continued within the Youghiogheny River Valley, the free-wheeling days were over for those desperadoes choosing to defy the legal system.

A Most Destructive Rain Storm

A S MOST western Pennsylvanians know the past couple years have been unusually rainy. Furthermore, those heavy rainfalls frequently have left the Youghiogheny River with swollen waters. And much of the overflow also occurs within the various tributaries, including Jacob's Creek. But such weather conditions have occurred many times over the centuries within the Youghiogheny River Valley. In July 1912, apparently, such a situation existed throughout the region. In fact, during the evening of July 17 [Wednesday], a cloudburst hit the Youghiogheny Valley with devastating results.

By all accounts, during the past three months, there had been severe storm almost daily. Accordingly, the river channels were unusually high for that time of year. And the high waters apparently had damaged the Baltimore and Ohio Railroad's wooden trestle which spanned the mouth of Jacob's Creek several miles from West Newton. Being a two-track railway many freight, and passenger trains passed over that span every day.

About 5:30 P.M. a large freight train originating in Connellsville was heading northward to Pittsburgh. Most of the cars were full of coke loads produced from the numerous "beehive" oven around Connellsville. Everything seemed to be normal as the train approached the eastern abutment of the trestle. No observer seemed to realize that the abutments had been significantly weakened after days of being battered by the high water. In any case, the engine and several front cars already had crossed the trestle without incident. The engineer recalled that the firemen suddenly yelled that the trestle was collapsing as the middle cars were passing over. Accordingly, eight cars, full of coke, tumbled into the Youghiogheny. Since none of the brakemen were on those cars, therefore, no one was injured. Several crewmen watched all this far to the rear within the caboose.

A reporter for the McKeesport *Daily News* declared, "Had a passenger train been crossed over the structure too it would have been sent crashing into the river . . . with a great loss of life." A Baltimore and Ohio official surmised that several days would be required to clear the wreckage, and repair the trestle. Meanwhile, a large amount of coke was floating down the Youghiogheny. Some pieces of coke were pulled from the driftwood within the vicinity of McKeesport.

In any case, until the needed repairs were completed traffic upon the Baltimore and Ohio would be problematic. A reporter for the *Daily News* stated: "As the result of the damage . . . trains on the B & O are coming late into this city and leaving over the tracks of the Pittsburgh and Lake Erie Railroad." Consequently, on Friday morning [July 20] a large group of McKeesport residents commenced a long-planned excursion to Atlantic City, New Jersey, aboard a special train charted from the Baltimore and Ohio. They were obliged, therefore, to travel on a Pittsburgh and Lake Erie train to Connellsville. At that point, they were slated to board a Baltimore and Ohio train, bound for Cumberland, Maryland. But that part of the journey also ran into difficulties. The heavy rains had caused a cave-in of the Sand Patch Tunnel in Somerset County. Subsequently, at

Meyersdale, they transferred to a Western Maryland Railroad locomotive heading into Cumberland. All told, they had been obliged to travel on three separate railway lines to reach that city. Apparently, the weary sojourners ultimately reached Atlantic City on another. Baltimore and Ohio train.

By all accounts, that monster storm had wreaked havoc throughout the Youghiogheny River Valley. The high waters had forced the closing of all the coal mines along the river. Telegraph and telephone were down throughout the region, thereby disrupting all outside communications. And eight persons reportedly drowned in the flooding near West Newton. A local farmer, Jon Raymond, living adjacent to Barron Run, a Youghiogheny tributary, went out into the storm to retrieve some grazing cattle. Upon failing to return Raymond's wife, mother, four children, and brother-in-law all went looking for him. Unfortunately, all of them were swept away when Barron Run suddenly overflowed. Over the next several days their bodies eventually were recovered at different points along the Youghiogheny.

About the only positive result about his deluge was it caused the end of a sweltering heat wave. Consequently, clear weather, and cool temperatures existed over the region as the resident cleaned up all the damage. By a journalist noted, "Warmer weather is on its way, though, and it will be only a few days will be clinging . . . in old-fashioned style."

Clairton and the Coke Industry

DURING THE decades following the Civil War, a longstanding occupation within western Pennsylvania suddenly became outdated. For centuries brawny workmen, known as puddlers, had played a vital role within iron industrial operations by manually stirring out ore impurities, notably sulfur and phosphorus, within large vats of boiling water. With the use of oxidizing substances, puddling was the process by which pig iron was converted into wrought iron. Not surprisingly, a puddler's work was quite labor-intensive, and time-consuming. By 1868, though, some enterprising operators along the Youghiogheny River were implementing a new industrial process that ultimately forced many puddlers into unemployment.

The Youghiogheny River Valley lay adjacent to a deep underground trough of rich bituminous [soft] coal running throughout the region. Consequently, numerous coal companies had established slope mining operations along the Youghiogheny. A pair of entrepreneurs, Abraham Tinstman and Colonel A.S. M. Morgan had formed the firm of Morgan and Company in Connellsville, Pennsylvania. Being coal miners, they were eager to utilize their commodity to create a revolutionary new substance that some observers were calling "coke." This sobriquet was derived by contracting two words, coal and cake.

They had begun using the "beehive oven" process which produced coke, a pure form of carbon possessing a smokeless, intense heat. The process had gained that name because the coal was converted into coke within large brick ovens shaped like beehives. Initially, coal was deposited into the "beehives" by lorry cars running along a track above a row of them. Subsequently, the coal was dropped into the front of each oven. Once the coal was inside, therefore, the openings were sealed with bricks. The coal was cooked into coke for about two days. During this period all the impurities, namely phosphorous and sulfur, were burned away. Upon being pulled from the oven this pure substance was watered down, and broken into small gray cakes. The coke eventually was shipped, either by river barges or railcars, to the Pittsburgh industrial mills converting iron into basic steel.

By 1872, Morgan and Company had constructed 111 beehive ovens along the Youghiogheny near Connellsville. Because the river often experienced low water levels, incapable of floating barges, the partners preferred shipping coke by the Pittsburgh and Connellsville Railroad. Moreover, they constructed similar beehive ovens further downriver, including one at Douglass Station in Elizabeth Township. Their coal was obtained from the various mines operating locally.

Unfortunately, though, the "Long Depression" of the 1870s ruined the solvency of Morgan and Company. By October 1875, a rising local entrepreneur, Henry Clay Frick, had acquired a controlling interest in the company. Frick already had opened his own coke works, consisting of fifty beehive ovens, upon 128 acres of land at Broadford, in June 1872. He could expand the coke production facilities through the timely financial backing of Judge Thomas Mellon, a leading Pittsburgh banker. He continued to operate those beehive ovens in Elizabeth Township.

Frick purchased a local railroad spur line which soon was connected to the Pittsburgh and Connellsville Railroad. Subsequently, Frick and Mellon helped arrange for the Baltimore and Ohio Railway Company to acquire the existing line. Meanwhile, the Frick Coke Company was operating 44,000 beehive ovens, especially in Westmoreland and Fayette Counties. Various commentators began referring to the entire territory as the "Connellsville Coke Region."

Not surprisingly, Frick soon became associated closely with Andrew Carnegie, the leading Pittsburgh steel magnate. In fact, Frick's coke enterprise became a subsidiary of the Carnegie Steel Company. By 1894, Frick was the sole coke supplier to Carnegie's various mills which dominated the Monongahela Valley. At that point, the two men decided that Frick's coke operations should be located upon the Monongahela River near Pittsburgh.

While pursuing this plan Frick became aware of a sizeable land tract in Mifflin Township, across the river from Elizabeth. Initially, Allegheny County officials had been planning to purchase 263 acres of that tract from a local realtor. They were planning to place the Allegheny County Almshouse upon that landholding. But that endeavor had been forestalled by 1895. Interestingly, the almshouse originally was to have been built on the Monongahela near the town of Munhall. Andrew Carnegie, however, had purchased the site to erect his Homestead Steel Works.

Meanwhile, near his prospective coke works, Frick had begun purchasing local real estate without much public notice. Two miles above this tract, Crucible Steel Company had been planning to construct a steel mill at West Elizabeth. Frick utilized his considerable fiscal resources, though, to incorporate that plan within his own project. Most of the bottomland belonged to J. Wylie Patterson, a prominent local farmer, whose family had owned that property for several generations. After purchasing

Patterson's landholding, Frick began buying up the adjoining acreage owned by the Large family. Many residents were not happy to discover that Frick had bought the apple orchards sitting upon the hill above the Wylie farmlands. And he was going to build his mill directly upon a popular riverside picnic area, Union Grove. Accordingly, this stretch of the Monongahela would be losing its pastoral atmosphere.

The name of Frick's new industrial plant would be known as the St. Clair Steel Company. This name apparently was selected in honor of Samuel St. Clair, the original owner of the lands where the mill was to be built. Samuel St. Clair had owned much of that area when Allegheny County had been established in 1788. Initially, the mill only was to include open-hearth steel furnaces. By 1901, Frick had also decided to erect three blast furnaces. Moreover, the St. Clair Terminal Railroad Company constructed a track network within the mill yard which was to connect with the nearby Pennsylvania Railroad. And a trestle was constructed across the Monongahela to make a connection with the Pittsburgh and Lake Erie Railroad running along the opposite bank. Upon building a loading dock for the incoming coal barges, Frick began implementing his plan for the coke-making plant. After this large coke plant began operations the beehive ovens around Connellsville were abandoned.

Frick also created the St. Clair Improvement Company which was established to build a town for the mill employees and their families. The new town was named Clairton and stood above the works. Accordingly, Clairton is the sole town in the Monongahela Valley which does not occupy any bottomland directly upon the river. By 1905, borough incorporation was granted to Clairton as the population increased with the plant's steady expansion. During the next two decades, this growing municipality annexed the neighboring hamlets of Blair, Wilson, Coal Valley, and Pine Run. Those towns had existed long before

Frick had contemplated his coke works. By 1930, Clairton was among Allegheny County's four incorporated cities.

As Frick was planning his model town the expanding industrial plant was coming under new ownership. For two years approximately the powerful New York banker, John Pierpont Morgan, had been negotiating with Carnegie to purchase his massive steel conglomerate. A master of "finance capitalism," Morgan was in the process of consolidating the steel industry throughout North America. He was attempting to end the endless, wasteful competition between the respective major steel corporations. Upon acquiring Carnegie Steel Company and its holdings for $400 million, in February 1901, Morgan had accomplished this goal.

Being a Carnegie subsidiary, H.C. Frick Coke Company was included within that transaction. Consequently, the new plant became part of the United States Steel Corporation, and gained the permanent name of Clairton Coke Works. For much of the 20th Century, thirteen percent of the coke produced globally originated within this facility. Unfortunately, though, during the last two decades of the past century. Clairton Coke Works underwent a substantial reduction in production capacity. And the inevitable cutback in the workforce had a negative impact on the local economy. Clairton Coke Works, however, remains among the few steel mills operating within the Monongahela Valley. Anyone traveling along the river still is able routinely to observe towboats pushing loaded coal barges into the landing beside the mill.

In any case, the multitude of abandoned beehive ovens within the "Connellsville Coke Region" fell into ruin. This writer, though, recently observed a row of those ovens, enveloped with vegetation, not far from Scottdale, Pennsylvania. The old ovens in Elizabeth Township were demolished about sixty years ago. Those structures located upon the Youghiogheny had become a hazardous playground for local children. The myriad of cyclists and hikers traveling along the adjoining Mon-Yough Trail have no idea that a successful coke-making operation ever existed nearby. At this point, the natural beauty of this trail is a world away from the plumes of industrial smoke issuing forth from the Clairton Coke Works smokestacks. Yet a definite connection does exist between these two diverse locales.

A Notable Scion of the Monongahela Valley

AMID THE final decades of the 19th Century, western Pennsylvania experienced considerable industrial growth. Within the upper Youghiogheny Valley, Henry Clay Frick had consolidated the coke industry, thereby becoming an important component of the regional economy. By 1892, Frick had merged his coke enterprise into Andrew Carnegie's large steel corporation operating nearby to Pittsburgh. By combining all the steps of the steel making process, Carnegie Steel Corporation had become the lynchpin of a vertically integrated industry. Throughout this process, Frick and Carnegie had retained the legal services of a leading Pittsburgh attorney, Philander C. Knox. During his long career, moreover, Knox served within the cabinets of three Republican presidents. This formidable lawyer also was a Monongahela Valley native.

Philander Chase Knox was born, on May 6, 1853, in Brownsville, Pennsylvania, then an important port town upon the Monongahela. Because his father, David S. Knox, was a prominent local banker, he grew up within an affluent household. Upon completing his education at Mount Union College in Alliance, Ohio, Knox decided to pursue a legal career. During his years at Mount Union, he already had cultivated a friendship with William McKinley, then a local attorney. After studying law within the offices of Henry S. Swope in Pittsburgh, he was admitted to the Allegheny County Bar in 1875. Furthermore, he established a law partnership with James H. Reed in Pittsburgh a couple of years later. The firm of Knox and Reed [now Reed Smith LLP] became well-known for specializing in corporate law. When creating his "steel empire" Andrew Carnegie frequently had the firm on retainer. As his legal career prospered, in June 1880, Knox married Lillian Smith of Pittsburgh.

Meanwhile, Knox was gaining a national reputation for his legal skills. While serving as the president of the Pennsylvania Bar Association in 1897, President William McKinley approached him about serving within his cabinet as Federal Attorney General. At that juncture, though, Knox was involved heavily in achieving an intricate corporate merger. Andrew Carnegie had agreed to sell his company to J. Pierpont Morgan, who was organizing a new corporation ultimately known at the United States Steel Corporation.

At the beginning of McKinley's second term, in March 1901, Attorney General John W. Griggs submitted his resignation. Upon this occasion, however, Knox agreed to accept this appointment. By April 9, he had begun his official duties. Knox was tending to personal business in Pittsburgh on September 14, when President McKinley was assassinated in Buffalo, New York. Although they were never close personally, Knox agreed to remain in office under President Theodore Roosevelt. Despite longstanding ties with many leading business executives, Attorney General Knox supported Roosevelt's decision to initiate a series of anti-trust corporate lawsuits.

In January 1903, at Roosevelt's instruction, Knox went to France and investigated the fiscal soundness of the Panama Canal Company. While in Paris he held a series of meetings with the company president, Phillipe Bunau-Varilla. Although wary of him personally, he did find that the French company was solvent. Consequently, Knox recommended that the United States purchase the Panama "concession." for $40 million. During the next decade, he was involved personally with many of the developments associated with the Panama Canal's creation.

With the death of U.S. Senator Mathew Quay of Pennsylvania, on May 28, 1904, Governor Samuel W. Pennypacker appointed Knox to serve out the unexpired term. Two years later the state legislature elected him to a full senatorial term. That action occurred during the final years before the direct popular elections of federal senators [17th Amendment] gained constitutional ratification. He became the Senate Rules Committee's chairman, and an important member of the Judiciary Committee. Nonetheless, he resigned his seat in 1909, to serve as secretary of state under President William Howard Taft.

Unlike the cool relations with Roosevelt, Knox was President Taft's good friend. By all accounts, Knox proved to be the most influential member of Taft's cabinet. And Secretary Knox handled his diplomatic duties capably. Not surprisingly, in 1912, Knox loyally supported Taft when Roosevelt challenged him for the Republican presidential nomination. The Republican schism, though, assured the victory of Woodrow Wilson, the Democratic candidate.

Upon leaving office, in March 1913, Knox returned to his legal practice in Pittsburgh. He sat on the boards of various corporations, including United States Steel and the Pittsburgh National Bank of Commerce. Growing bored with practicing law, though, he was eager to reenter electoral politics. Furthermore, he made no secret of his strong dislike for President Wilson. Accordingly, in November 1916, Pennsylvania voters popularly elected him to the U.S. Senate.

Upon assuming his seat, Knox became an important member of the Senate Foreign Relations Committee. He strongly supported, in April 1917, the entrance of the United States into World War I. Although supportive of most war measures, Knox's interactions with President Wilson were minimal. Following the war's conclusion, on November 11, 1918, rumors were circulating that Senator Knox would be among the official delegation accompanying Wilson to the international peace conference in Paris. But Wilson summarily dismissed such talk.

Through his overseas contacts, however, Knox was aware of the various developments within the negotiating sessions. After the Treaty of Versailles was signed, on June 28, 1919, Knox finally read the final draft. While not opposed generally to the Versailles Treaty, he was wary of the provision calling for the creation of the League of Nations. He promptly argued that the League of Nations should have been the subject of a separate treaty. Like many of his senatorial colleagues, he would have supported the treaty, providing certain "reservations" were incorporated. But the obdurate Wilson did not contemplate any modifications to the Versailles Treaty, which was submitted, on July 10, for senatorial ratification. Apparently, Wilson ignored Knox's request for a personal interview.

By March 19, 1920, the U.S. Senate twice had failed to ratify the Treaty of Versailles. On both occasions, Knox cast a negative vote. During the autumn of 1919, Knox had become aware of reports that the president had experienced a serious illness. He did not know, though, that Wilson had suffered a severe stroke. In any case, Knox submitted a joint resolution calling for a separate peace treaty with Germany. This congressional measure was not enacted while the Wilson administration remained in power. The separate German peace treaty did not get through Congress until July 1921. The new Republican president, Warren G. Harding, promptly signed the treaty into law.

On October 12, 1921, Senator Knox, after participating within a Senate floor debate, returned to his office suite to dictate some correspondence. He left his chambers in apparent good health. While strolling down the hallway, though, Knox suddenly suffered a massive stroke. He was declared dead within several minutes. Following a public funeral in Washington, D.C., his remains were conveyed to Pennsylvania for final burial,

Philander Chase Knox was interred privately within a family plot on his country estate at Valley Forge. Several weeks later, however, Knox's old western Pennsylvania friends held a public memorial service at Sixth Street Presbyterian Church in downtown Pittsburgh. A comparable service was held in his honor within his old hometown of Brownsville. Those were the people who had known him the longest and best.

About the Author

MILES RICHARDS is a retired history educator currently residing in McKeesport, Pennsylvania. He received his Bachelor of Arts from Edinboro State University. With a longstanding interest in western Pennsylvania he was a charter member of the Elizabeth Township Historical Society. He later moved southward to pursue graduate studies in history at the University of South Carolina. Upon gaining a PhD at the University of South Carolina in 1995, he began a teaching affiliation with Midlands Technical College in Columbia. During those years he wrote regularly for various historical publications, including a monograph, *Remembering Columbia South Carolina: Capital City Chronicles* (2007). Upon returning to western Pennsylvania he resumed his interest in regional history, especially around the Youghiogheny and Monongahela Rivers which converge at McKeesport. For the past decade he has written monthly historical features for variousl local newspapers. He has been teaching history courses for the Osher Lifelong Learning Institute at the University of Pittsburgh. He has spoken at a number of local historical and civic groups. He is excited about writing his first book on his native region.